The Pedant's Revolt

The Pedant's Revolt

Why Most Things You Think Are Right Are Wrong

ANDREA BARHAM

Michael O'Mara Books Limited

First published in Great Britain in 2005 by
Michael O'Mara Books Limited
9 Lion Yard
Tremadoc Road
London SW4 7NQ

This updated paperback edition published in 2011

A CIP catalogue record for this book is available from
the British Library

ISBN: 978-1-84317-587-2

1 3 5 7 9 10 8 6 4 2

www.mombooks.com

Designed and typeset by E-Type
Illustrated by Andrew Pinder

Printed and bound in Great Britain by
CPI Cox & Wyman, Reading, RG1 8EX

For my sister, Lynsey, with love.

New occasions teach new duties:
Time makes ancient good uncouth;
They must upward still, and onward,
Who would keep abreast of Truth.

The Present Crisis,
James Russell Lowell,
(1819–91)

Contents

Acknowledgements

I would like to thank Andy Barham, Simon Blackman and Andy Jerrison for being lovely, and for giving me practical book-writing help. I am indebted to all the experts who humoured me by answering my questions, without whom there would be no book. Thank you to Jennifer Blackman for the emergency loan of her chair, and a big thank you to my editor, Helen Cumberbatch, who put (nearly) as much fervour into this book as I did.

Foreword

We are all, nowadays, bombarded with facts and figures, but how many of them are accurate? Have you ever stopped to wonder? *The Pedant's Revolt* is for everyone who wants to throw out received wisdom and welcome in the facts.

For example, on one occasion I revealed to a friend that one's heart stops when one sneezes. My friend asked, 'Is that actually true?' 'Apparently,' I replied. Then I looked it up and discovered that it wasn't true. This made me wonder how many more 'facts' I thought I knew were, in reality, spurious: can owls really turn their heads all the way round? Can one get high on aspirin and Coca-Cola? And can hair really turn white over night?

The bug had bitten. Each answer threw up more questions and revealed more misconceptions, so I began to collect them. When I reached five hundred I started to wonder if *anything* I believed was true. I discovered that Hitler *wasn't* a vegetarian, Cleopatra *wasn't* Egyptian and Easter *isn't* named after a pagan goddess.

I learned that, over time, truth is sometimes corrupted; conjecture can become mistaken for fact; nonsense somehow becomes enshrined in the annals of our collective received wisdom. I wondered how so much misinformation had got around, and I have come to the conclusion that things get repeated not because they are based upon truth, but because they *sound* good. How many people have regaled you with the fascinating 'fact' that we swallow eight spiders a year in our sleep? The spider myth is recent, but fallacies such as 'ostriches stick their heads into sand' date back to ancient Rome. Some can be traced back to a specific reference, such as a painting in the case of the Roman thumbs-down gesture, and even a film in the case of the 'lemmings commit suicide' misconception.

The strength of belief in fallacies can be awesome: there are statues erected to non-existent heroes such as the 'little Dutch boy', Hans Brinker, and there are events attributed to the wrong person, like Dick Turpin for example. Even great ancient historians such as Suetonius and Dio can't always be relied upon to keep to the facts.

Today, with Internet access to such works such as the *Encyclopaedia Britannica* and the Oxford reference collection, it has never been easier to find things out. It seems the further we progress into the twenty-first century, the less people are willing to accept old wives tales and urban myths and the more willing they are to find out the truth for themselves: a development of which I wholeheartedly approve.

1
Art, Literature and Entertainment

Harpo Marx was mute

Adolph Arthur Marx, known as Harpo Marx, was perfectly able to speak. He was also a talented and self-taught harpist, which is how he got his nickname.

In November 2000, Radio Two's *The Birth of Screen Comedy* featured Harpo's son Bill Marx explaining why his father suddenly stopped speaking on stage. It came about as a result of a bad review, which said that 'his pantomime was wonderful, but when he opened his mouth to speak he ruined the image'. According to Bill Marx: 'Dad took it to heart and he just stopped talking.'

You can hear Harpo Marx explaining how he fell off a stool while playing the harp in a brothel at the following website: www.marx-brothers.org/living/harposp.htm

Toulouse-Lautrec was a dwarf

The French artist Toulouse-Lautrec may have been born with a congenital disorder, but it wasn't achondroplasia (dwarfism) as is commonly believed. Arnold Matthias, author of *Henri de Toulouse-Lautrec*, has discovered that it was much more likely to have been 'a hereditary bone disease (pyknodysostosis)'.

The *Encyclopaedia Britannica* reveals that at the age of thirteen, Toulouse-Lautrec broke his left thighbone, and just over a year later he fractured his right thighbone in a second mishap. The resulting damage caused to his bones left his legs atrophied and made it very difficult for him to walk. According to the findings of geneticist Philip R. Reilly, in his book *Abraham Lincoln's DNA and Other Adventures in Genetics*, as an adult Toulouse-Lautrec 'stood just shy of 4 feet 11 inches tall'.

A further misconception surrounding the artist concerns the name 'Toulouse'. Often regarded as his first name, Toulouse actually formed part of his surname. The *Encyclopaedia Britannica* cites his full name as 'Henri-Marie-Raymonde de Toulouse-Lautrec-Monfa'.

Errol Flynn was Irish or English or American

Dashing Hollywood actor Errol Flynn earned acclaim as a great swashbuckler in films such as *The Adventures of Robin Hood* (1938) and *The Sea Hawk* (1940). Biographer Jeffrey Meyers reveals in his 2002 book *Inherited Risk* that in an effort to perpetuate Flynn's romantic screen image, Hollywood publicity departments portrayed Flynn as a 'mad Irishman', an 'elegant Englishman' and a 'bold American'.

However, Meyers reliably informs us that Flynn was the son of Australian scientist, Professor Theodore Leslie

Thomson Flynn, and he was born 'on the cold, strange island of Tasmania' in 1909. Therefore Flynn was neither Irish, English nor American, but Australian by birth.

Humpty Dumpty was an egg

Humpty Dumpty came to be regarded as an egg after he was drawn as one in Lewis Carroll's 1872 children's book, *Through the Looking-Glass*. Before that, no one knows for sure exactly what Humpty Dumpty was.

In *The Great Plague*, writer and historian A. Lloyd Moote suggests that Humpty Dumpty was 'the royal cannon ... that fell from a church wall [St Mary at the Walls, Colchester, Essex] during a Civil War siege' in the late 1640s.

Don't worry gentlemen, fortunately I'm not an egg.

Legend has it that a Parliamentary cannon ball hit the tower wall below where the royal cannon was positioned, which caused it to fall off. All the King's horses (the horsemen) and all the King's men (the foot soldiers) tried to raise Humpty Dumpty on to another part of the wall, but failed.

Though many believe this story to be true, there's no proven connection between the cannon and the nursery rhyme.

Walt Disney is cryogenically frozen

The US film producer, director and animator Walt Disney is, of course, the most famous cryogenically preserved celebrity. At least, he would be if he had really been frozen. Disney hated funerals and before he died he made it clear that he did not wish to have one. Consequently his funeral service in December 1966 was small and private. Less than a month later, local psychologist Dr James Bedford became the first person to be preserved at the Cryonics Institute, Michigan, USA. The fact that the birth of cryonics and Disney's low-key funeral occurred at much the same time seems to have been the main reason why questions were raised about the final resting place of Disney's body.

The printed version of the rumour is said to have first appeared in the French magazine *Ici Paris* in 1969. It was then mentioned in a number of unauthorized biographies, one of which, Marc Eliot's *Walt Disney: Hollywood's Dark Prince*, also claimed that Disney had an interest in cryonics. So was Walt Disney frozen? Not according to the Cryonics Institute who have stated: 'We don't think so.'

Biographers Katherine and Richard Greene, who had full

access to the Disney family and archives have said in their 1998 book *The Man Behind the Magic: The Story of Walt Disney*: 'Contrary to rumour, Walt was cremated – not frozen.' Indeed, his death certificate states that his remains were subject to a 'cremation' on '12/17/66' at Forest Lawn Memorial Park, Glendale, Los Angeles, California, after which, according to *Frommer's Los Angeles 2004* author Matthew Richard Poole, they were buried 'in a little garden to the left of the Freedom Mausoleum'.

Did you know . . . ?

'Walking in the Air', the theme song from the 1982 children's animated adventure *The Snowman,* about a boy who makes a snowman on Christmas Eve, was a big hit for Aled Jones in 1985, and reached number five in the UK charts in December.

However, it's not Jones's voice on the film soundtrack: it was St Paul's Cathedral chorister Peter Auty. His name didn't appear on the original film credits, but has now been properly acknowledged on the latest version.

Victorian actress Sarah Bernhardt performed wearing a wooden leg

The nineteenth-century French actress Henriette-Rosine Bernard (aka Sarah Bernhardt) certainly lost a leg during the course of her long career. During a South American tour in 1905, she sustained an injury to her right knee while appearing in a production of the play *La Tosca*, when she landed badly after jumping off the parapet in the last scene of the play. Ten years later the leg had become gangrenous and had to be amputated. Bernhardt was seventy-one years old.

Though Bernhardt did try using a prosthetic leg, she didn't take to it. However, she was determined not to let this setback damage her successful acting career, and when she was able, she embarked on another European tour in 1920, in which she played roles that she could act while remaining seated.

The theatre critic Howard Greer describes one of Bernhardt's valiant performances in an article published in the *Theatre Magazine* in 1920: 'Throughout the action of the play the star [Bernhardt] makes but two appearances and remains seated upon her golden palanquin. She is carried upon the stage by four richly armoured slaves and reclines voluptuously on her cushions.'

'Puff, the Magic Dragon' is a veiled reference to smoking marijuana

Legend has it that this delightful children's hit song by US folk group Peter, Paul and Mary is all about smoking marijuana: i.e. 'Puff' refers to drug-related smoking; 'little Jackie Paper's' surname implies cigarette-rolling papers; 'autumn mist' is marijuana smoke; and the land of 'Honalee' refers to the Hawaiian village of Hanalei, famed for its highly potent marijuana plants. However, this suggestion has been strongly denied by all those associated with the song's origins.

Leonard Lipton, author of the original 1959 poem that formed the basis of the song, has claimed that it was

Yeah, I'm Puff, now beat it, kid.

inspired by Ogden Nash's poem 'The Tale of Custard the Dragon', and was about the transition from childhood to adulthood. While the song's co-writer, Peter Yarrow, has added: 'When "Puff" was written, I was too innocent to know about drugs . . . What kind of a mean-spirited SOB would write a children's song with a covert drug message?'

What kind indeed? Anyone want to cast aspersions on Peter, Paul and Mary's second hit 'Blowin' in the Wind'?

W. C. Fields has 'I'd rather be in Philadelphia' on his tombstone

It is often claimed that US actor and screenwriter W. C. Fields – who starred in films such as *My Little Chickadee* (1940) and *Never Give a Sucker an Even Break*

(1941) – has the above legend engraved on his tombstone. In fact, the brass plaque in Forest Lawn Memorial Park, Glendale, Los Angeles, California which marks his final resting place simply reads: 'W. C. Fields 1880–1946.'

Biographer James Curtis explains that the famous epitaph – 'Here lies W. C. Fields. I would rather be living in Philadelphia' – which is often misquoted, first appeared in *Vanity Fair* in October 1924. Fields made the quip in response to the journalistic question: how would you like your epitaph to read? The quote is often paraphrased as: 'On the whole, I'd rather be in Philadelphia' or 'All things considered, I'd rather be in Philadelphia'.

Frankenstein was a monster

Mary Shelley's Gothic horror story *Frankenstein* is named after the main character Victor Frankenstein, who creates a monstrous living being out of human body parts. English professor Ellen Moers's commentary, *Female Gothic*, explains that 'the scientist runs away and abandons the newborn Monster, who is and remains nameless.' Therefore, the creature should be properly referred to as 'Frankenstein's monster'.

Incidentally, Frankenstein wasn't a German doctor, but a Swiss student of natural science.

2

Things That Are 'Bad' For You

Chewing pencils causes lead poisoning

In a recent column in a national broadsheet newspaper, I was interested to read about a 'homeopathic dowser healer' who claimed that Princess Diana had once suffered from lead poisoning, which had affected her posture. The Princess was quoted as recounting an incident when, as a schoolgirl, the point of a lead pencil had 'broken off into her face'. The healer was able to 'extract the poison', which apparently led to an improvement in the Princess's posture.

The only problem with this miraculous cure is that, as historian Christian Warren points out in his book *Brush with Death*, pencil lead 'is not lead at all, but graphite'. The misnomer dates back to the Middle Ages, when the newly discovered mineral 'graphite' was nicknamed 'German lead'. Pencils don't and never have contained lead.

As for being poisoned by pencils, *Poisons Quarterly* states categorically that there is 'no risk of developing lead toxicity from chewing pencils'.

Children of first cousins will be physically or mentally impaired

There has long been a Western taboo about the act of marriage between first cousins: in an estimated thirty US states the practice is illegal. More precisely, though, it's generally the prospect of the resulting offspring that fills people with dread.

In the eighteenth and nineteenth centuries, the existence of haemophilia in the European royal families was often cited as an example of why cousins marrying was a bad idea. However, genetic counsellor Robin L. Bennett points out in an article in the *Journal of Genetic Counselling* that 'the inheritance of this X-linked recessive condition [haemophilia] would have occurred regardless of the consanguineous unions [cousins' intermarriage] in the royal families.'

It appears that the fear surrounding the taboo dates back to nineteenth-century research which exaggerated the risk of children of cousins being born with birth defects. In *Forbidden Relatives*, anthropology professor Martin Ottenheimer points out that in a study of the children of blood-related couples in rural Sri Lanka, scientists found 'no significant decrease in offspring viability'. Provided small, isolated communities are taken out of the equation, Ottenheimer suggests that 'modern research does not confirm the common notion that first-cousin marriage represents a significant physical threat to the offspring'.

Medical anthropologist Dr Alison Shaw agrees that 'birth incidence data suggest the risk of having a child affected by a genetic condition is about two per cent . . . in first-cousin couples the risk doubles to about four per cent'.

That leaves ninety-six out of a hundred cousin-couples with healthy children. Though Ottenheimer points out that a risk to the offspring of close consanguineal relatives still exists, it would appear to be considerably smaller than many people think.

Close work and reading in dim light damages eyesight

It's a common belief that 'over-using' one's eyes will somehow wear them out. Oddly, no similar claims are made for 'too much listening', 'too much tasting' or 'too much touching' causing damage to the relevant organ or limb.

Assistant Professor of Ophthalmology at the University of Arkansas for Medical Sciences, Dr Nicola Kim, tells us that, as a rule, your eyes can't be damaged by normal, everyday use:

There are a few specific exceptions, like looking directly into sunlight and laser light, but other than this, reading in dim or bright light will not change the health or function of your eyes . . . It may feel more difficult to focus if the lighting is suboptimal [less than ideal], but this has no permanent effect on the structure of your eyes. Likewise, sitting too close or too far from the TV will also have no permanent effect on your vision.

Childcare expert Dr Spock has also stated that children's eyes are not harmed either by being near to the TV, 'reading an excessive amount, reading in poor light, or holding the book close'.

Equally, as Dr Robert Mendelsohn writes in *How to Raise a Healthy Child*, 'there is no scientific evidence that . . . reading in a moving vehicle . . . exposure to flashbulbs and strong artificial light . . . wearing another person's glasses . . . or going without your glasses will damage your eyes'. In fact, in his book *Bad Medicine* science writer Christopher Wanjek has expressed the belief that in the modern world there are only a few everyday activities that will lead to vision loss.

It seems that many adults believe they are somehow to blame for being short-sighted and fear the same fate for their offspring. Perhaps this fallacy has grown from people's propensity to blame themselves for some of their physical shortcomings rather than accept the fact that they started out that way. Besides, if sitting too close to a TV screen or computer monitor really could damage eyes, most IT workers would be finding their way round with white sticks by now.

Knuckle-cracking causes arthritis

Can knuckle-cracking really lead to arthritis or does your mum just tell you that to scare you into stopping making the annoying noise? In 1990, J. Castellanos and D. Axelrod published their findings from a study of 74 knuckle-crackers and 226 non-knuckle-crackers aged forty-five years or over and revealed that there was 'no increased preponderance of arthritis of the hand in either group'.

Author of *All About Bone* Dr Irwin M. Siegel states:

In an otherwise healthy hand, 'cracking' the knuckles is not hazardous and does not cause arthritis . . . Some scientists think that the 'cracking' or 'snapping' sound is caused by a ligament, tendon, or joint capsule sliding over a bony protuberance . . . Others trace the popping to the bursting of gas bubbles that are released when the joint is stretched, reducing pressure on its contained synovial fluid.

From the results of a 1995 study, published in the *Journal of Manipulative & Physiological Therapeutics*, R. Brodeur did warn, however, that in the process of cracking one's knuckles 'it would be difficult to generate the forces in the appropriate tissue without causing muscular damage'. So it would seem that although knuckle-cracking may not damage any bones in the hand or lead to the development of arthritis, it may cause some long-term damage to the soft tissue, which is probably worth bearing in mind as you contemplate unleashing another satisfying 'snap' from a beleaguered pinky.

Powdered glass is an effective 'poison'

Powdered glass: the Victorian standby method for doing away with annoying relatives. The only trouble is, it doesn't work.

I haven't tried it out myself, but I know of a man who did. Seventeenth-century physician and writer, Sir Thomas Browne tells us in his 1642 publication *Pseudodoxia Epidemica*, 'That Glass is poison, according unto common conceit, I know not how to grant . . . from experience, as having given unto Dogs above a dram thereof, subtilly [*sic*] powdered in Butter and Paste, without any visible disturbance.'

So there we have it: Dr Thomas Browne tried to poison some dogs with it, only to discover that it didn't work. And they say the standard of medical ethics is slipping . . .

Dr D. P. Lyle, the author of the more recently published *Murder and Mayhem*, points out that 'very fine glass is unlikely to cause any lethal damage to the GI [gastro-intestinal] tract ... Even with coarser glass, the bleeding would probably not be massive or life-threatening, but slow and lead to anaemia and fatigue.'

Larger glass shards are another matter entirely, but most victims won't be too keen to munch even a slightly gritty lunch – if you've ever eaten a sandwich on a beach on a windy day, you'll know what I mean.

Blunt knives and scissors are safer than sharp ones

It's true that sharp scissors and knives can be dangerous (particularly in the wrong hands), but blunt ones can cause even more damage. As a keen crafter in my youth, I used to be issued with only the bluntest of blunt knives and scissors to work with on my projects, presumably to reduce the chances of my suffering any painful mishaps. Despite this supposed precaution, on many occasions I nearly cut off a finger attempting to force a blunt blade through fabric or card.

In *The Outdoor Survival Handbook*, survival expert Raymond Mears explains that a blunt knife 'requires more pressure behind it to cut, and it tends to slip on the surface it is cutting, rather than biting in like a sharp knife'.

Judy Walker of Cutco Cutlery confirms that 'sharp knives are safer because less pressure is required to cut through food', and though it's always advisable to avoid any knife-related injuries, she also points out that 'if you manage to cut yourself, at least it'll be a clean cut'.

Sitting on hot or cold surfaces causes haemorrhoids

I wonder how 'old wives' hit upon the idea that sitting on wet grass could result in haemorrhoids. A wet bottom, yes – but haemorrhoids?

The belief may be due to the fact that, according to *The Family Encyclopedia of Medicine and Health*, 'internal haemorrhoids [piles] used to be thought of as varicose veins,' which may have prompted the notion that an increase in circulation (brought about by sitting on hot surfaces) or a decrease in circulation (effected by resting on cold surfaces) would give rise to the condition. *The Family Encyclopedia of Medicine and Health* explains that haemorrhoids are now considered to be 'spongy tissue rich in small blood vessels'.

Indeed, BBC Radio Four *Case Notes* presenter Dr Mark Porter condemns the former belief as 'rubbish', revealing that the two biggest causes of haemorrhoids are 'constipation and pregnancy'.

3

Of Biblical Matters

Eve gave Adam an apple in the Garden of Eden

Genesis 3:6 tells us: 'And when the woman saw that the tree was good for food, and that it was pleasant to the eyes, and a tree to be desired to make one wise, she took of the fruit thereof, and did eat, and gave also unto her husband with her; and he did eat.' The type of fruit is never specified. Not here, or anywhere else in the Bible.

In his book *The Second Jewish Book of Why*, Rabbi Alfred J. Kolatch explains that: 'Although in the Christian tradition the forbidden fruit in the Garden of Eden is the apple ... in Jewish tradition it is the fig, since the leaves from which Adam and Eve made aprons (girdles) to cover their nakedness were taken from the fig tree mentioned in the very next chapter.'

Jonah was swallowed by a whale

In Jonah 1:17 we read: 'Now the Lord had prepared a great fish to swallow up Jonah. And Jonah was in the belly of the fish three days and three nights.'

Every schoolchild knows that a whale is a mammal not a fish. Indeed, most whales, although they can grow to enormous proportions, have very small throats. Even killer whales would not be able to swallow whole anything bigger than a small seal.

Perhaps Jonah was swallowed up by a really big haddock . . .

Onanism is a biblical term for masturbation

One of the less savoury Old Testament stories concerns the 'sin of Onan', which has come to be regarded as the sin of masturbation, for which Onan was punished by death. However, the story related in Genesis 38 reveals a sin of a somewhat different kind.

Judah told Onan to marry his dead brother's wife and 'raise up seed to thy brother', but Onan wasn't overly enthusiastic about the idea, even though, in accordance with Hebrew customs, a man was expected to marry his deceased brother's wife if she was still childless at her husband's death, and the first-born son of this union would then be regarded as a legal descendant of the dead man.

The story continues that 'Onan knew that the seed should not be his; and it came to pass, when he went in unto his brother's wife, that he spilled it on the ground, lest that he should give seed to his brother. And the thing which he did displeased the Lord: wherefore he slew him.'

It appears that to avoid giving an heir to his dead brother's estate, Onan practised *coitus interruptus* – the withdrawal method of contraception during intercourse –

thereby deliberately failing to impregnate his new wife and former sister-in-law as instructed.

Thus, the sin of Onan wasn't masturbation, but a deliberate attempt to break with Hebrew traditions using non-reproductive intercourse, which Onan duly paid for with his life.

Did you know . . . ?

The actions of Delilah, the infamous biblical temptress, were certainly a key factor leading to Samson's loss of strength, but she did not cut off his hair herself.

Judges 16:19 tells us that 'she called for a man, and she caused him to shave off the seven locks of his head; and she began to afflict him, and his strength went from him.'

So it would seem that Delilah did not cut off Samson's hair directly: she got a man in to do the job for her.

In the Gospel, Jesus said, 'It is more blessed to give than to receive'

In Acts 20:35, Paul tells us to 'remember the words of the Lord Jesus, how he said, 'It is more blessed to give than to receive.'

Worthy sentiment though it is, and doubtless Jesus would have believed this, it appears that there is no reference to him ever having said this in any gospel writings.

4

Birds and Insects

Migratory birds fly south during winter to escape the cold

Many people believe that if migratory birds remain in the north during winter months they will die from the cold, but this is not the case.

Ornithologist Paul Kerlinger points out in his book *How Birds Migrate* that 'many species can tolerate cold temperatures if food is plentiful; when food is not available they must migrate.'

According to environmentalist Alon Tal, birds' feathers are 'sufficiently warm to allow them to maintain their high body temperature and survive the winter'. However, when temperatures drop below 10 degrees Celsius, insects – a major food source for birds – are barely active, and the frozen earth makes it difficult for the birds to dig around to find their usual food supplies. Therefore, Tal concurs that migratory birds fly south in the winter not because of the cold, but 'to find food'.

Ducks' quacks don't echo

This modern myth has found its way on to BBC TV and radio programmes *Shooting Stars* and *Home Truths*.

Its like is generally spread by 'did-you-know?' sites on the Internet and is a good example of how misleading trivia can gain momentum by constant repetition – regardless of whether it is true or not.

Professor Trevor Cox sets us straight. In 2003, Cox placed Daisy the Duck in an 'echo' chamber to prove that ducks' quacks do indeed echo. With an MP3 player, it is possible to listen to Daisy's quack echo at www.acoustics.salford.ac.uk/acoustics_info/duck/?content =index/.

So how did the widely believed myth arise? According to Cox, a duck's quack has a 'gentle decay', which causes its echo to fade very quickly, making it really difficult to discern.

Quite how someone initially witnessed a seemingly non-echoing duck quack, and spread word of the imagined phenomenon, is another matter entirely.

Homing pigeons use a mysterious form of navigation

Loft-reared pigeons that are driven hundreds of miles away and then released can somehow find their way home. But how do they do this? Are their methods so unfathomable that they are shrouded in mystery? No, is the simple answer to that question.

In his 1971 study 'Magnets Interfere with Pigeon Homing', using somewhat unusual techniques involving the glueing of magnets on to the backs of pigeons, William T. Keeton describes how when the birds were released into a heavily overcast sky they became disoriented, but that 'no such disorientation occurred during similar releases under clear skies'. Keeton concluded that pigeons find their way home by noting the position of the sun and detecting subtle variations in the earth's magnetic field to work out which way is north. In other words, they use inbuilt 'compasses'.

Best avoid the motorway on a bank holiday.

However, in 1997 T. Burt's research team reported that when pigeons fly over familiar territory they navigate by sight. By 2004, animal behaviourists at Oxford University led by Professor Tim Guilford had discovered that pigeons follow a map: a road map.

The amazing findings were featured in a *Daily Telegraph* article in February 2004, in which Guilford commented: 'If they have made the journey before, the pigeons are more likely to say, "Well, I know this is south – the way I want to be going – but rather than fiddle around with my inbuilt compass I'm going to follow the A34, which will take me home nicely."'

Not such bird-brains, then.

Guilford remarked how it was 'almost comical' following the progress of one group of birds that was released near a major A road: 'They followed the road to the first junction where they all turned right, and a couple of junctions on, they all turned left.' One bird even flew down a road and circled a roundabout, before choosing to take another turning, presumably giving way to any fellow pigeons approaching from its right.

At least there are no traffic jams in the sky.

Moths eat clothes and mothballs should be used to ward them off

Whenever I saw a moth flitting round my bedroom I used to panic, thinking it would be into my cupboards and munching away at my woollies as soon as my back was turned, but then I found out that the type of moth that eats clothing very rarely flies, and besides, as consumer adviser Debra Lynn Dadd points out, in her book *Home Safe Home*, 'It is the larvae of these moths that eat fabric, not the moth itself.'

So even if you do find *tineola bisselliella* – a skinny little silvery-gold chap that scuttles about at the back of your cupboards – he's harmless by the time he's pupated . . . until he finds a mate, that is.

There once was a time when mothballs were the thing to discourage moths setting up home in your cupboards and laying eggs in your clothes – and they used to be very useful – but nowadays, as author Jane Hersey warns, mothballs (naphthalene or para-dichlorobenzene) are no longer a good choice because they won't necessarily stop at poisoning moths. In *Why Can't My Child Behave?*

Hersey warns: 'Infant deaths have been reported after the babies were simply exposed to blankets and clothing which had been stored with mothballs.'

In place of mothballs, Dadd advises that 'herbal repellents are very effective . . . lavender, rosemary, mint, and peppercorns all repel moths, but the classic repellent is cedar.'

Ostriches bury their heads in the sand

For centuries the ostrich has been ridiculed for symbolizing the folly of being in denial. Ancient natural historian Pliny the Elder started the smear campaign in the first century, saying of the animal that 'the veriest fooles they be of all others'. However he didn't, as often reported, declare that ostriches thrust their heads into sand. That's daft because they would surely suffocate. What Pliny actually said was: 'They thrust their head and necke once into any shrub or bush, and get it hidden, they thinke then they are safe ynough, and that no man seeth them.'

Ostrich expert and author of *Dreambirds*, Rob Nixon, having observed the birds in the wild, explains what really happens: 'When danger threatened, the ostrich hen would . . . sit dead-still . . . flattening her endless neck . . . against the earth . . . A flattened ostrich blends easily into the dry Karoo bushes which, for most of the year, are greyish humps of dead-looking sticks.'

So, ostriches aren't refusing to face up to the inevitable, they are simply doing a jolly good impression of a bush.

Owls can turn their heads right the way round — through 360 degrees

Grizzly ancient folklore stated that if you circled an owl in a tree, the bird would watch you walk round and round the tree, turning its head until, eventually, it would wring its own neck. They certainly had some curious means of entertainment back in those days. It's true that owls cannot move their eyes in their sockets, and so instead they have to turn their heads. However, they cannot rotate them all the way round.

Canadian ornithologist, the aptly named Professor David Bird, explains in *The Bird Almanac* that owls have 'a system of well-developed cervical vertebrae and neck muscles', which allows them considerable flexibility when moving their heads. However, they are only able to turn their heads a maximum of 270 degrees.

You've been roosting on that roundabout again.

Female mantises always eat their partners after mating

Mrs Mantis has had a bad press. She is famed for eating her partner after mating and her apparently gruesome exploits have often been showcased in wildlife documentaries.

However, according to biologist Tom Wakeford, in his 2001 book *Liaisons of Life*, more methodical studies have shown that such behaviour was not typical of the mantis species, explaining that this sort of cannibalism was 'brought on by the extremes of stress that frequently exist under laboratory conditions'. It's not surprising – you're in a strange place, you don't much like the look of the grub, some bloke leaps on you . . . Would we humans react any differently if we had the same head-munching abilities?

Michele Doughty, student at Bryn Mawr College, conducted a less stressful mantis-mating experiment. Her 2002 paper, *The Female Praying Mantis: Sexual Predator or Misunderstood?*, revealed that 'out of thirty matings, we didn't record one instance of cannibalism . . . instead we saw an elaborate courtship, with both sexes . . . stroking each other with their antennae before finally mating. It really was a lovely display.' Ah, how romantic!

Commenting on the 1935 study of mantis behaviour by physiologist Kenneth Roeder, entomologist and author May R. Berenbaum claims that it was these findings which are 'widely credited with suggesting that sexual cannibalism is required among mantids [mantises] . . . Roeder didn't really go so far as to suggest that decapitation was a necessity. He was the first to admit that the conditions under which he made his observations were, to say the least, artificial.' In *Buzzwords* Berenbaum also reports that 'later studies failed to document cannibalism at all.'

As a point of interest, Roeder's theory ran that the head of the male *had* to be bitten off by the female to prompt sperm release. Apparently, this does not hamper the mating process because the male's reproductive system is not controlled by the head. A universal truth, perhaps?

On average, people swallow eight spiders per year in their sleep

This scary urban legend has doubtless kept many arachnophobes awake at night. However, Rod Crawford, the Curator of Arachnids at Burke Museum in Seattle, believes that the notion has no basis in fact. He explains: 'For a sleeping person to swallow even one live spider would involve so many highly unlikely circumstances that for practical purposes we can rule out the possibility . . . No such case is on formal record anywhere in scientific or medical literature.' It might be reassuring to hear that in the seventeen months that Rod Crawford's Spider Myth website has been online he tells us 'I have not heard from a single person claiming that a spider entered their mouth.'

Indeed, the myth was debunked decades ago in a 1954 book called *Insect Fact and Folklore*, in which the author Lucy Wilhelmine Clausen refuted the belief that people swallow spiders while asleep.

So how did the spider-swallowing myth resurrect itself so successfully in the twenty-first century? It appears that in 1993, a columnist for US computing magazine *PC Professional*, Lisa Holst, wrote an article called 'Reading is Believing', in which she complained about the lists of spurious 'facts' circulating on the Internet. To illustrate her point, Holst invented her own list of falsehoods, which included the fallacy referred to in Clausen's book that, on average, people swallow eight spiders per year in their sleep.

Presumably, the image evoked such a strong reaction in people that speedy repetition spread it throughout the world even though it wasn't true, which thereby proves Holst's point about the prevalence of sham 'facts' on the Internet.

Science has proven that bumblebees are aerodynamically unable to fly

But, of course, bumblebees can and do fly, and not because they are performing a miracle, but because we had our sums wrong. The myth dates back to a calculation made by French mathematician André Sainte-Laguë in 1934. French entomologist Antoine Magnan gave ill-advised credence to the mathematician in his book *The Flight of Insects,* in which he claimed that the size and shape of the humble bumblebee made their ability to fly impractical: 'Influenced, initially, by aviation studies, I applied the laws of air resistance to insects, and arrived at the same conclusion as M. Sainte-Laguë: that their flight was impossible.'

However, it transpires that Sainte-Laguë's calculations hold water only for stationary wings such as those of aeroplanes. Bees, which are more like helicopters, beat their wings rapidly, and it is this motion that enables them to fly, regardless of their physique.

If a baby bird is handled the mother will 'smell a human' on it and reject it

Setting the record straight, the Royal Society for the Protection of Birds (RSPB) states that 'touching a bird will not make the parents abandon it . . . Birds have little or no sense of smell.' Ecologist David Mizejewski supports this view in his book *Attracting Birds, Butterflies, and Other Backyard Wildlife*: 'The adult won't reject the baby because of human scent . . . most birds have a poor sense of smell and won't even perceive human odour.'

In fact, such is their underdeveloped sense of smell that, according to biologist Marlene Zuk, in most cases parents would even continue to feed an alien nestling if it happened to be mistaken for one of their own.

If a young bird is found alone on the ground, the RSPB points out that we should not automatically assume that it has been abandoned: 'It is really best not to interfere. The parents will be close by and come to feed the bird as soon as it is safe.' However, if the bird seems to be in a vulnerable position, the RSPB confirms that 'it will do no harm to move it into shelter, but not too far away as the parents will then be unable to find it.'

Some spiders are deadly

Arachnophobia – fear of spiders – is very common, but though spiders might look sinister, the truth is they are generally quite harmless. Spider expert Rainer F. Foelix reveals in his book *Biology of Spiders* that 'statistically, spider bites are much less dangerous to man than the poisonous stings of bees, wasps, and hornets,' which is due to the fact that a spider's poison is primarily designed to paralyse its prey.

With regard to the much feared tarantula, despite its size it is much less dangerous than is commonly thought. According to Foelix: 'the ancient fear of their poisonous bite has been proven to be quite wrong.'

Fellow spider expert Rod Crawford agrees:

> There is no spider species anywhere that can properly be called 'deadly' . . . I know of no species anywhere on earth capable of causing death in humans in as much as ten per

I know of no species anywhere on earth capable of causing death in humans...

cent of cases, even if untreated . . . If the person bitten obtains medical aid, death from a genuine spider bite . . . is . . . a decided rarity worldwide.

So much for the notion of 'deadly' spiders that can incapacitate an unsuspecting person in minutes – Crawford reassures us that they are found 'only in the movies'. What a relief!

5

William Shakespeare

'Brevity is the soul of wit' means 'Don't take too long to tell a joke'

This saying is endlessly quoted in all those 'How to be a best man' books and comes from Shakespeare's *Hamlet* (Act II, Scene 2).

Addressing Hamlet's mother, Lord Polonius says, 'Therefore, since brevity is the soul of wit, / and tediousness the limbs and outward flourishes, / I will be brief: your noble son is mad.'

But where's the joke? The fact is, there isn't one, because in the context of the play, Polonius wasn't making the point that it's better not to take too long to tell a joke – wise words, though they may be.

When Shakespeare wrote the line in the 1600s, 'wit' also meant 'wisdom'. In fact we still use expressions such as 'slow-witted', 'witless' and 'dimwit', and yet none of these expressions have anything to do with humour. What the expression actually meant was that 'a wise speaker does not require long-winded explanations,' and so he had got to the point quickly in order to tell the queen that her son was mad.

There is a joke, though, for those familiar with the play and its characters. It lies in the fact that long-winded speeches are exactly what Lord Polonius ends up making; of brevity, there is usually no sign.

'Salad days' are carefree days of youth

If we think back to our 'salad days' with fondness, then really we shouldn't. In Act I, Scene 5 of *Antony and Cleopatra*, Cleopatra declares, 'My salad days, / When I was green in judgement: cold in blood, To say as I said then!'

Clearly, Cleopatra's salad days were a time when she was raw and green: naive and inexperienced. We can almost sense her cringe when she thinks back to the way she was years ago.

When Juliet asks, 'Wherefore art thou Romeo?', she is trying to locate her lover

In spoof stagings of the balcony scene in *Romeo and Juliet* (as well as in some genuine ones), Juliet stands on her balcony (even though the text stipulates that she appears 'at a window') and searches, hand shading her eyes (even though it's night), for her beloved.

However, 'wherefore' means 'why', not 'where'. The meaning is clearer in the context of a line in Act I, Scene 1 of *Julius Caesar*: 'Wherefore rejoice? / What conquest brings he home?' Indeed, we still retain the meaning in the expression 'the whys and the wherefores'.

Juliet isn't trying to locate her beloved: in fact, she doesn't even know he's out there. Juliet is merely wailing to herself through a window (like you do): 'O Romeo, Romeo! wherefore art thou Romeo? / Deny thy father and refuse thy name; / Or, if thou wilt not, be but sworn my love, / And I'll no longer be a Capulet.' She moans on: ''Tis but thy name that is my enemy; / – Thou art thyself, though not a Montague.'

If Romeo weren't from the 'enemy' Montague family, poor thirteen-year-old Juliet's romance would be going a lot more smoothly.

Wherefore art thou Romeo?

'Discretion is the better part of valour'

Shakespeare penned this often quoted expression the other way round.

The reference appears at the end of *Henry IV, Part One* (Act V, Scene 4), when Falstaff, feigning death, mutters,

'The better part of valour is discretion', adding, 'in the which better part I have saved my life.'

The wordplay hinges on the two 'betters', not the 'valour'.

'It's all Greek to me'

'It's all Greek to me' is often uttered to convey the notion that something is too difficult to understand. The correct version of the phrase is first mentioned in Act I, Scene 2 of *Julius Caesar*. Casca, one of Brutus's co-conspirators, is asked by Cassius what the great orator Cicero had said during a recent public gathering, but Casca couldn't elaborate, such was his ignorance of the foreign language:

Cassius: Did Cicero say any thing?
Casca: Ay, he spoke Greek.
Cassius: To what effect?
Casca: Nay, an I tell you that, I'll ne'er look you i' the face again; but those that understood him smiled at one another and shook their heads; but, for mine own part, it was Greek to me.

'Methinks, the lady doth protest too much'

In this misquoted phrase the words tend to be repeated in the wrong order.

In Act III, Scene 2 of *Hamlet*, when Hamlet asks his mother how she had liked the stage play they had been watching (which had cleverly mirrored recent dastardly events in the royal household), the Queen refers to the part of the Player Queen (a parody of herself), and replies, 'The lady doth protest too much, methinks.'

'Alas, poor Yorick. I knew him well'

In Act V, Scene 1 of *Hamlet*, the Prince of Denmark is in a churchyard with his friend Horatio, and finds himself reminiscing about the king's jester, Yorick, whose skull he holds in his hands: 'Alas, poor Yorick! I knew him, Horatio – a fellow of infinite jest, of most excellent fancy.'

Doubtless Hamlet did know Yorick well when the jester was alive, but he never once says this throughout the play, despite the popular misquotation.

6

Customs and Beliefs

Aryans were an ancient race of tall, blue-eyed blonds

According to Indology lecturer and writer Edwin Bryant, it was a German philologist by the name of L. Geiger who, in 1878, was the first to suggest that the Indo-Europeans were 'blond, blue-eyed people'. In *The Quest for the Origins of Vedic Culture*, Bryant explains how Geiger suggested that 'these traits had become diluted and darkened in those places where there had been a foreign admixture of genes: "The Indo-Germanic people remain unadulterated wherever pure blond traits are best preserved."'

Geiger's notions later became popular with the Nazi Party: in a 1929 Nazi propaganda leaflet 'Aryans' were described as 'tall, long-legged, slim ... the skin is rosy bright and the blood shines through ... the hair is smooth, straight or wavy; the colour is blond.'

However, the true Aryan race were a people who spoke an Indo-European language and who, in prehistoric times, settled in Iran and northern India in the second millennium BCE. On the tomb of King Darius I (521–485 BCE), at Naqsh-i Rustam, near Persepolis, it is proclaimed: 'I am

Darius . . . a Persian [Iranian], son of a Persian, an Aryan, having Aryan lineage.'

Therefore one can only assume that Geiger's prehistoric 'blond, blue-eyed' Aryans must have also had very large prehistoric sun hats.

'An eye for an eye' justifies personal vengeance

The *Encyclopaedia Britannica* reveals that in ancient Babylonian, biblical, Roman, and Islamic law, the eye-for-an-eye principle was 'operative in private and familial settlements, intended to limit retaliation, and often satisfied by a money payment or other equivalent.'

Biblical scholar Donald A. Hagner points out in his commentary *Matthew 1–13* that 'the *lex talionis* [an eye for an eye] is presented more as a way of limiting the degree of personal vengeance that one may take upon another, than as a positive teaching about what a person must or should do.'

In *Hot Issues*, author Mark Ashton confirms that 'In the law of Moses, the "eye for an eye" command . . . was there as a limit on the amount of damages for which a wronged person could sue.'

Therefore, the ancient law of *lex talionis* appears to have been designed to make the punishment fit the crime, to ensure that no victim could then demand the death of the perpetrator for a minor offence.

Before Columbus, everyone believed the world was flat

The fifteenth-century Italian explorer Christopher Columbus was said to have amazed incredulous churchmen when he returned from his explorations and announced the world was round. Except that – they already knew. As geologist Dr Cesare Emiliani explains in *Planet Earth*, as early as 500 BCE, 'Pythagoras ... claimed that the Earth was a sphere.'

First-century natural historian Pliny the Elder, writing in *Natural History* on 'the forme of the earth' noted 'by a generall consent we doe all agree ... [about] the round

49

ball of the earth . . . that it is a globe enclosed within two poles.'

Astrophysicist Marc Lachieze-Rey also points out that thirteenth-century English mathematician and astronomer John of Holywood (aka Johannes de Sacrobosco), in his work *On the Spheres of the World*, stated that the earth 'in several ways must be a sphere'.

So much for Columbus's astonishing 'revelation'.

In Japan, the extended family uses the same bath water in which to wash

This practice sounds like something that families would be forced to do during a drought, when water supplies are severely restricted. Fortunately, there is nothing unhygienic about the way that the Japanese share their bathwater. As Leonard Koren, author of *How to Take a Japanese Bath*, explains: 'The act of scrubbing the body free of dirt always takes place outside the tub. Only after the body is clean does the bather finally enter the water.'

In *The Art of the Bath*, writer Sara Slavin describes the traditional way that 'Japanese bathers "shower" before their bath, so they don't contaminate the bathwater with soap and grime,' which is similar to the protocol of cleaning oneself before using a communal jacuzzi or hot tub.

Author of *The Japanese Dream House*, Azby Brown, adds that because a Japanese bath is used essentially for soaking, 'it can easily be used by several bathers and even for successive days'.

Hence the saying that 'Westerners bathe to get clean, but the Japanese get clean to bathe.'

Easter gets its name from a pagan goddess

The eighth-century chronicler Bede, in *De Ratione Temporum*, claimed that the word 'Easter' came from the Anglo-Saxon goddess of spring and fertility, Eostre or Eostrae. The *Encyclopaedia Britannica* disputes this notion, stating that: 'Given the determination with which Christians combated all forms of paganism, this appears a rather dubious presumption.' Rather, it is widely believed that 'the word derives from the Christian designation of Easter week as *in albis*'.

If you can't see the connection that's because it hinges on a mistranslation. German scholar J. Knoblech explains:

Among Latin-speaking Christians, the week beginning with the Feast of the Resurrection was known as hebdomada alba *[white week], since the newly-baptized Christians were accustomed to wear their white baptismal robes throughout that week. Sometimes the week was referred to simply as* albae *[white].*

According to Knoblech, when the word was translated into German, it was mistaken for the plural of *alba* meaning 'dawn', and so the 'white' connection was forgotten: 'They accordingly rendered it as Eostarum, which is Old High German for "dawn".' And thus came the word 'Easter' in English.

Priests have always been celibate

In *The Oxford Companion to British History* John Ashton Cannon points out that 'clerical celibacy, common since early Christian times, has scant scriptural authority.'

Charting the history of church development in *The Western Church in the Middle Ages*, author John A. F. Thomson suggests that celibacy became policy in the eleventh century, when 'Alferd Lanfranc of Canterbury . . . at the Council of Winchester in 1076 . . . laid down that while priests should be forbidden to marry in future, those who had wives should not be required to put them away.'

It was made official in the twelfth century, as Robert A. Burns (author of *Roman Catholicism After Vatican II*) reveals: 'Two Church councils, Lateran I in 1123 and Lateran II in 1139, made clerical celibacy a universal law, which has remained.'

Pagans are devil-worshippers

Lexicographer John Ayto reveals that the word 'pagan' originally meant 'something stuck in the ground, a landmark' and later came to mean 'country dweller'; it has certainly no links to Satan or the Devil.

Authors of *A History of Pagan Europe* Prudence Jones and Nigel Pennick point out that 'the idea of a Devil, a subverter of the One Truth, is not found in Paganism.'

The *Encyclopaedia Britannica* further backs up this view with the following explanation: 'Modern witchcraft and neopaganism are not to be confused with Satanism . . . These groups worship not Satan, but pre-Christian gods.'

In her 1994 book *Celebrate the Earth*, 'High Priestess of witchcraft' Laurie Cabot states emphatically that 'there is no Devil or Satan in our religion'.

Satan is a Judeo-Christian and Islamic concept with no connection to older pagan practices.

Limbo is a 'waiting room' for Heaven

The word 'limbo' does not appear in the Bible. It is of Teutonic origin and means 'border'. According to the *Encyclopaedia Britannica*, in Roman Catholic theology, it is 'the border place between Heaven and Hell where dwell those souls who, though not condemned to punishment, are deprived of the joy of eternal existence with God in Heaven'. The concept of limbo probably developed in the European Middle Ages.

The Reverend Peter M. J. Stravinskas says, 'It is the state or place, according to some theologians, reserved for the dead who deserved neither the beatific vision nor eternal punishment . . . however . . . no official teaching ever advocated this notion.'

The *Essential Catholic Handbook* tells us that 'a rather common theological opinion has been that infants who die without baptism are excluded from Heaven, but spend eternity in a state of natural happiness called limbo,' although such a theological explanation has 'never been explicitly taught by the Church'.

The state of limbo seems to be often confused with that of Purgatory, which is the place for those who have died in God's grace, having repented of (but not expiated) their sins, whose souls require purification before entering Heaven.

Popes have always been infallible

In Catholic theology, the issue of papal infallibility means that when the Pope makes a statement on a matter of faith and morals, which either reiterates what has always been taught by the Church or concerns *ex cathedra* solemn definitions (which can never contradict what has formerly been taught), his word is final and true and cannot be corrected.

Far from having a long history in the papacy throughout the centuries, Richard McBrien, author of *Lives of the Popes,* reveals that 'it was Pius IX who . . . called the First Vatican Council (1869–70), which defined the . . . infallibility of the pope.'

7

Drink

Drinking a cold beer on a hot day quenches thirst

During hot weather, people often cite the high temperature as the reason for downing as many cold beers as possible, but according to the findings of Professor Eric Klinenberg, which feature in his book *Heat Wave*, this is not such a good idea: 'Drinking alcohol is particularly dangerous during hot summer weather because it contributes to dehydration.'

Dr Robert H. Shmerling claims that drinking a chilled lager may actually make you more thirsty. He explains that although the beer provides fluid, because alcohol 'inhibits the brain's release of ADH ... [antidiuretic hormone] the kidneys no longer hold on to water as well as they did before you drank the beer', which means that your kidneys are prompting you to pass more water than usual. Therefore, if you drink beer on a hot day, Shmerling warns that 'there is the real possibility that your dehydration will worsen rather than improve.'

Drunk drivers cause most
road accidents

According to the findings of the THINK! road-safety campaign: 'Seven per cent of all road casualties and fifteen per cent of deaths in 2002 occurred when someone was driving when over the legal limit for alcohol.'

Alcohol, therefore, certainly causes dangerous driving on the nation's roads but the National Youth Agency points out that a larger percentage, namely 'twenty per cent of all serious road accidents,' are caused by tiredness. The Royal Automobile Club (RAC) states that 'Government research has suggested that as many as ten per cent of all road casualties and twenty per cent of all motorway accidents are caused by drivers who fall asleep whilst driving.'

THINK! also reveals that 'twenty per cent of accidents on long journeys on trunk roads and motorways' are

caused by drivers 'falling asleep at the wheel'. The Royal Society for the Prevention of Accidents (RoSPA) adds that 'on motorways and trunk roads a quarter [twenty-five per cent] of all crashes that caused death or serious injury were sleep related'.

Thus, these statistics strongly suggest that tiredness causes more road accidents than drink-driving.

Coffee sobers up a drunk

Healthcare organization BUPA tells us that 'the body can only metabolize [break down] alcohol at a fixed rate. Broadly speaking, this is about one unit (eight grams) per hour.' There are two units in a pint of beer, so if you drink five pints it will be ten hours before your blood alcohol level is back down to zero.

The Surrey Alcohol and Drug Advisory Service (SADAS) points out that 'time is the only factor in the action of the liver removing alcohol from your body'. Coffee cannot speed up the sobering-up process. Nothing can. SADAS states that 'coffee will only wake you up, so you have a wide-awake drunk instead of a sleepy drunk'. Likewise, a cold shower will make you a wet drunk and a run round the block will make you a tired drunk.

Combining Coca-Cola and aspirin induces a 'high'

In his book *Secret Formula*, author Frederick L. Allen dates this myth all the way back to the early 1930s, when an Illinois doctor wrote to the *Journal of the*

American Medical Association to warn of a new craze among teenagers who were 'dissolving aspirin in Coca-Cola to create an "intoxicating" beverage with addictive properties that were as bad as "narcotic habituation"'.

There's nothing like telling teenagers not to do something, and the fact that it doesn't actually work doesn't seem to have deterred them through the years.

BBC Radio Four *Case Notes* presenter Dr Mark Porter suggests the result of mixing aspirin and Coca-Cola wouldn't be intoxication, but rather a bout of 'indigestion'. Pharmacologist and author of *The Aspirin Handbook* Joe Graedon is in full agreement: 'There is no way you can get high on aspirin and Coke.'

St Bernard dogs used to carry brandy flasks

What is the St Bernard dog most famous for? Carrying a brandy keg round his neck, of course. In reality, however, as dog breeders George and Maureen Gwilliam point out in their book *New Saint Bernard*, St Bernards never did carry brandy barrels. The travellers' hospice at the St Bernard Pass, between Switzerland and Italy, did exist, and St Bernard dogs were certainly used to help find lost travellers, but the trusty canines were never equipped with casks of reviving spirit.

It would appear that the myth dates back to the work of the Victorian painter Sir Edwin Landseer. In *The Atlas of Dog Breeds of the World*, canine experts Bonnie Wilcox and Chris Walkowicz reveal that Landseer included the 'whimsical addition' of the brandy cask in his 1820 painting *Alpine Mastiffs Reanimating a Distressed*

Traveller, with the result that 'Landseer's . . . non-existent brandy flask has carried through the years.'

Red wine should be uncorked or decanted to allow it to 'breathe'

The art of wine appreciation is often riddled with mysticism. In *How to Taste: A Guide to Enjoying Wine* expert Jancis Robinson comments that 'many ordinary wine drinkers claim that some wines, especially cheap reds, taste much better if opened and not decanted, but simply left to "breathe" for a few hours.' She goes on to remark that 'in such circumstances the wine can take only the most minimal of "breaths", and any change is bound to be imperceptible' since 'the surface area of wine exposed to the air is so small that the effects of any aeration are negligible.'

Writing in his 2003 *Pocket Wine Guide*, fellow wine expert Oz Clarke agrees: 'Scientists have proved that opening young to middle-aged red wines an hour before serving makes no difference whatsoever . . . The surface area of wine in contact with air in the bottle neck is too tiny to be significant.'

Is decanting a better option? Robinson points out that the 'traditional but disputed reason for decanting is to promote aeration and therefore encourage the development of the wine's bouquet', and quotes 'scientifically respectable' Professor Emile Peynaud as saying that 'the action of oxygen dissolved in a sound wine is usually detrimental.' His advice is to 'decant only wines with a sediment, and then only just before serving'.

If there is an improvement in taste after uncorking or

decanting, Robinson suggests that this is because 'with very cheap wines there may be off-odours trapped in the gap between the surface of the wine and cork ... this "breathing" process allows them to evaporate.'

So, if your red wine smells good, you can pour it straight from the bottle, but if it's a bit stinky, it's better to air it till the whiff improves. Mystic? Sounds like common sense to me.

Did you know ...?

The Tea Council reveals that 'a 190ml cup of tea contains 50mg of caffeine, one third less than the same amount of an instant cup of coffee (75mg).'

Author of *Tea: Addiction, Exploitation and Empire* Roy Moxham explains that 'leaf tea contains about two to four per cent caffeine ... twice as much as in coffee beans,' but because a smaller weight of tea is needed to make up a cup, the caffeine content duly falls to less than that in an average cup of coffee.

8

Food

Chocolate triggers migraines

Chemicals in chocolate such as caffeine, phenylethylamine and theobromine are often blamed for causing migraines. Indeed, C. M. Gibb's 1991 research team found that 40 per cent of subjects who believed chocolate caused their migraine had an attack after eating it.

However, in double-blind studies, in which subjects don't know if they are getting the real preparation or a dummy one (which in this case was carob), results differed. In a 1974 study by researchers Moffett and Swash using eighty subjects, they found that 'only thirteen headaches occurred to chocolate alone,' which led them to conclude that 'chocolate on its own is rarely a precipitant of migraine.'

In a further double-blind study in 1997, D. A. Marcus's research team found that chocolate was no more of a culprit than the chocolate substitute, carob, in causing migraines or headaches. They concluded that 'contrary to the commonly held belief of patients and physicians, chocolate does not appear to play a significant role in triggering headaches in typical migraine, tension-type, or combined headache sufferers.'

And how about those who get tension headaches if they can't get their hands on some chocolate? Craving chocolate prior to a headache may be a symptom of the onset of the headache rather than the cause. NHS Direct Online explains:

> It is worth noting that some things that you may think are triggers (for example, chocolate), may have been a craving in the prodromal [early] phase [of the migraine]. This means that the migraine was on its way before you ate the chocolate, so the chocolate was not the cause.

I can feel a headache coming on – GET ME SOME CHOCOLATE!

Chewing gum takes seven years to pass through the body

Back in the 1860s, when latex chewing gum made from the sap of the sapodilla tree of Central America first appeared in the Western world, it was described as 'indigestible' and 'not meant to be swallowed'. Since that time, sinister reasons why this was so seem to have developed to replace the less than riveting fact that it simply wasn't ever intended to be swallowed.

So, does swallowed gum do ghastly things to our insides and hang around for years? 'Nonsense,' says presenter of BBC Radio Four's *Case Notes*, Dr Mark Porter, who estimates the time it takes for gum to pass through the body at 'more like twenty hours'.

Chewing-gum manufacturer Wrigley's describes the contents of the product, to set the record straight about the consumption of a piece of gum:

Chewing gum has five basic ingredients – sweeteners, corn syrup, softeners, flavours and gum base [the part that puts the 'chew' in chewing gum]. The first four ingredients are soluble, meaning they dissolve in your mouth as you chew. Gum base doesn't. And although it isn't meant to be swallowed, if it is, it simply passes through your system, just like popcorn or any other form of roughage. This normally takes only a few days.

Haggis originated in Scotland

In *The Oxford Companion to Food*, food writer Alan Davidson reveals that 'the first people known to have made products of the haggis type were the Romans.' In her book *The Haggis*, food writer Clarissa Dickson Wright reveals that renowned etymologist Professor Walter W. Skeat 'assigns a Scandinavian origin to the

Nooooooo!

word, with an Anglo-French suffix. The "hag" part is Scandinavian, and Skeat links it to Icelandic hoggva and haggw – to hew.' Cassell's *Dictionary of Word Histories* agrees, suggesting that the word 'haggis' derives from the Old Norse *hoggva*, meaning 'to strike with a sharp weapon', which relates to the chopped-up contents of the dish.

In his *Dictionary of Word Origins*, lexicographer John Ayto suggests that the word haggis derives from Old French *agace* which means magpie, because 'the collection of edible odds and ends a pie contained was similar to the collection of trinkets assembled by the acquisitive magpie.'

Sheep's innards and sparkly trinkets? I can't really see the link.

Honey is healthier than sugar

Nutritional experts in *The Encyclopedia of Foods* state that '"natural" sugars such as honey, maple syrup, date sugar, molasses, and grape juice concentrate have acquired the reputation, albeit incorrectly, of being healthier than sugar,' when in fact the truth is that 'these sweeteners contain no more vitamins or minerals than table sugar.'

The Institute of Food Science and Technology in London suggests that 'there is nothing especially healthy about honey. The traces of micronutrients it contains are too small to make any significant contribution to our diet.'

The Encyclopedia of Foods also adds a warning that honey may contain small quantities of the spores of the bacteria that produce botulism toxin, and therefore honey should 'never be given to babies younger than one year'.

Meat should never be eaten rare

Regarding the eating of whole cuts of meat that are cooked rare, the Food Standards Agency states that:

> [with] steaks, cutlets and joints, any bacteria are generally on the outside of the meat. If the outside is cooked, this should kill any bacteria, even if the middle of the meat is pink. This means you can eat whole cuts of beef . . . [and] lamb . . . when they are pink or rare, if you would like to.

It is important to be aware that different rules apply to minced-meat products, such as burgers and sausages. When these are made, bacteria are mixed right through in the mixing process, and so the Food Standards Agency warns us to 'cook sausages and burgers until any juices run clear and there's no pink meat left'. The same applies to poultry and game such as chicken, turkey, duck and goose.

Uncooked? With my stomach? Are you mad?

Spinach contains large amounts of iron and makes you strong

Professor Terry J. Hamblin set the record straight on spinach in the *British Medical Journal* (BMJ) in December 1981, where he explained that this myth dates back to a study by Dr E. von Wolf in 1870. Before the days of typewriters, von Wolf recorded his data by hand, and one day this led to a misplaced decimal point in his publication appearing to show that the iron content in spinach was ten times greater than in reality.

German chemists eventually corrected the error in 1937, but by that time, the idea had already taken hold, and probably gave rise to the legend of Popeye's spinach-guzzling strength which, of course, also served to reinforce the myth.

Spinach does contain some iron, but in her book *Food Folklore*, nutrition expert Roberta Larson Duyff explains that 'oxalic acid, another food component in spinach, binds with iron and limits its absorption.' And in any case, Duyff points out that 'physical exercise, not iron or any other nutrient, builds muscle strength'.

So spinach won't make you strong or able to lift heavy objects like Popeye, and it isn't the greatest iron source, but it is a rich source of vitamin A, E and several vital antioxidants.

'Welsh rarebit' is the correct term for cheese on toast

According to *Fowler's Modern English Usage*, Mrs Hannah Glasse first included a 'Welsh Rabbit' recipe in *The Art of Cooking* in 1725. (Apparently, she also called it 'Scotch Rabbit' on the same page. Eighteenth-century proofreading was clearly a hit-and-miss affair.)

No matter how we spell it, it's clearly vital we have a fancy name for the dish: 'cheese on toast' is just too dull.

9

Things That Are 'Good' For You

A hot toddy will keep out the cold

Cold weather isn't good for much, but it's often useful as an excuse to knock back a few spirits. However, this turns out to be rather a bad idea.

Medical journalist and broadcaster Dr Trisha Macnair explains that alcohol 'causes dilation of peripheral blood vessels, so increasing heat loss'. In other words, if you drink alcohol in cold conditions, rather than retaining heat your body pumps more blood to your hands and feet at the expense of your vital organs. You might feel warm (and you may even look flushed), but the precious heat being diverted to your extremities is then quickly lost in the surrounding cold. The heat you are feeling is the heat being lost from your body; the sensation of feeling warmed up is really an illusion.

Dr James A. Wilkerson also reveals how excess alcohol reduces heat generation by interfering with shivering, which is the natural way the body protects itself against the cold.

Chris Townsend, survival expert and contributor to the *Encyclopedia of Outdoor and Wilderness Skills*, warns that

I told him brandy wouldn't help.

far from keeping out the cold 'alcohol does just the opposite – in fact, it can even advance hypothermia'.

So although a few nips of brandy might seem like a good idea when you're stuck at the top of a snowy mountain in the middle of a blizzard, it's probably better to wait.

Cough medicine is effective

Two research groups recently studied the effectiveness of over-the-counter (OTC) cough medicine. In 2001, Dr K. Schroeder's team concluded: 'There is no good evidence for or against the effectiveness of OTC medicines in acute coughs.' They also made the valid point that the 'identification of ineffective preparations could avoid costs for consumers and healthcare providers'.

In 2003, Dr Ian M. Paul's team came to this conclusion:

Diphenhydramine and dextromethorphan are not superior to placebo [dummy preparations] in providing nocturnal symptom relief for children with cough and sleep difficulty as a result of an upper respiratory infection ... Furthermore, the medications given to children do not result in improved quality of sleep for their parents when compared with placebo.

Professor Alyn H. Morice, Head of the Division of Academic Medicine of the University of Hull, points out that although OTC cough preparations do 'appear' to reduce coughs, 'this effect is no greater than that seen with placebo.' Morice recommends that if one takes an OTC cough preparation, 'it should be of the simplest composition in order to minimize the risk of side effects.'

Dr Richard Russell of the British Thoracic Society said: 'Over-the-counter sales for acute cough medicines currently reach approximately £100 million a year in the UK – money that is being spent on remedies, where there is no evidence that they work.'

It sounds as though it makes more sense to stick with the old-fashioned combination of honey and lemon – at least it tastes nice.

Copper bracelets improve arthritis

The theory is that tiny amounts of copper from copper bracelets leach into the skin – leaving the tell-tale green tide-mark – and help regenerate cartilage. If arthritis sufferers opt to wear a copper bangle they are guaranteed the green mark which is produced by the copper reacting with acidic salts in their sweat, but what about the cartilage regeneration?

Dr Randy Bindra of the University of Arkansas for Medical Sciences points out that 'it's never been proven that copper can be absorbed through the skin by wearing a bracelet ... no modality of treatment has been shown to cure or reverse the changes of arthritis.' Bindra also adds that 'copper deficiency is extremely rare and most regular diets provide enough copper to meet the daily requirements.'

The Arthritis Research Campaign agrees: 'Research has shown that people with arthritis do have enough copper in their bodies for normal health. So it is difficult to understand what effect these bangles can have ... There is no research supporting the use of copper bangles.'

During exercise follow the dictums: 'no pain no gain' and 'go for the burn'

The 'no pain, no gain' maxim dates back to the late 1960s, when bodybuilders such as Arnold Schwarzenegger were 'pumping iron'. If you take 'no pain, no gain' to mean that a degree of effort is required to achieve a useful level of fitness, then fair enough, but if you interpret it as meaning running cross-country till your thigh muscles ignite, that's not so good.

In his book *The Maffetone Method*, athletics coach Dr Philip Maffetone blames the 'no pain, no gain' saying for many incidences of overtraining: 'According to this myth, you have to suffer, to exercise to the point of agony, in order to benefit from exercise ... Too many people begin an exercise programme with the clear intention of getting into shape only to get injured and never work out again.' Maffetone adds that it certainly isn't necessary to push yourself too far to get good results: 'If you never work out hard, you'll still reap great benefits. For example, dramatic benefits can be attained by easy walking for thirty minutes, five days per week.'

Author of *The Nine Truths About Weight Loss* Dr Daniel S. Kirschenbaum has described the dictum 'no pain, no gain' as 'both wrong and potentially dangerous': 'Your muscles should feel fatigued during the last repetitions, but you should not feel sharp or piercing pains in your muscles or joints.'

As for Jane Fonda's 'going for the burn', according to the healthcare organization BUPA, 'regular exercise is more important than strenuous exercise . . . If it hurts and you're out of breath, you're probably overdoing it.' BUPA also reveals that 'Jane Fonda admits that she was wrong about going for the burn.'

'No pain, no gain, no brain', perhaps? (Sorry, Jane.)

Eating a hot meal is beneficial, particularly during cold weather

When I swallow my food, I like it to be pretty much the same temperature as the rest of me: I find it's far less likely to scald my oesophagus that way. I blame certain breakfast cereal commercials for promoting the dubious practice of forcing hot porridge down unwilling school children.

The *Manual of Nutrition* (1985) produced by the then Ministry of Agriculture, Fisheries and Food (MAFF) states that 'the heat of hot food is trifling compared with the energy provided by metabolism of its constituents within the body.'

The publication also reveals that the 'heat' is 'perceived, and gives a useful boost to morale on cold days'. So it would appear, therefore, that the health benefits of a hot meal are primarily psychological, and it only feels as though it's doing us some good.

Large doses of vitamin C prevent the common cold

In 1970, US Nobel Prize-winner Linus Pauling advocated this method to ward off the common cold, and today, many people swear by mega-doses of vitamin C for protection against colds. However, though several large-scale studies have been conducted, no conclusive data has shown that large doses of vitamin C can indeed prevent colds. Indeed, vitamin C expert Professor Balz Frei of the Linus Pauling Institute in the United States has stated that there is 'no evidence . . . that vitamin C can lower the incidence of the common cold or prevent it'.

In 1991, A. B. Carr's research team analysed ninety-five pairs of identical twins who took part in a double-blind trial of vitamin C tablets. They concluded that 'vitamin C had no significant effect, except for shortening the average duration of cold episodes by nineteen per cent.'

In his 1997 paper on vitamin C and the common cold, researcher Tedros Amanios also points out that overall, in previous studies, vitamin C showed no marked effect on the occurrence of colds: 'Vitamin C does not appear to reduce the incidence of colds in "normal" people; it only decreases the incidence of colds in people who are under heavy physical stress.'

Dr Charles Born of the Medical Sciences Pharmacy at the University of Kansas warns that 'too much vitamin C can cause severe diarrhoea, a particular danger for elderly people and small children.'

No need to throw your vitamin C out, though, as Frei agrees with Carr that 'vitamin C can shorten the duration of the symptoms of the common cold by about twenty per cent' once you have already caught it. Amanios concurs: 'Since vitamin C seems to reduce the symptoms of colds, it is advisable that people use vitamin C during episodes of the common cold.'

Inhaling ozone is health-promoting

Ozone is created when an electric discharge is passed through oxygen. It gives that fresh smell on cotton sheets that have dried on the washing line on a windy day. However, the *Encyclopaedia Britannica* also describes it as an 'irritating, pale blue gas that is explosive and toxic, even at low concentrations'. Ozone is good in the upper atmosphere, helping to filter out UV radiation, but not so good when it builds up close to the ground in cities, hence the phrase 'ozone – good up high, bad near by,' although you wouldn't think it from the claims of air-purifier manufacturers who include 'ozone technology' in their products.

Victorian health fanatics are blamed for advocating the inhalation of lungfuls of ozone at the seaside. No doubt its presence on the coast made the sea air smell fresher, giving the impression that it was somehow healthier. However, the *National Cyclopaedia of Useful Knowledge* (1850) informed its readership (anecdotally, but correctly, as it turns out) that: 'The inspiration [i.e. inhaling] of ozone is very injurious . . . M. Schönbein [Christian Friedrich Schönbein discovered ozone in 1840] states that he was seriously affected by breathing an atmosphere charged with it.'

In *Life and Breath*, author Dr Neil Schachter warns that 'long-term repeated exposure to high levels of ozone may lead to large reductions in lung function, inflammation of the lung lining, and increased respiratory distress,' which is very far from health-promoting, no matter what the Victorians once thought.

'Hypoallergenic' pillows are recommended for asthma and allergy sufferers

According to the findings of researcher T. J. Kemp, which were published in the *British Medical Journal* in 1996, 'for many years asthmatic patients have been told to avoid using feather-filled pillows on their beds, although there is no evidence to support this practice.' In fact, Kemp's team discovered that 'polyester-filled pillows contained significantly more total weight of Der p I [dust-mite allergen] . . . and significantly higher μg Der p I/g [fine dust] than the feather-filled pillows.'

A year later, B. K. Butland's team of researchers found that 'use of non-feather pillows was positively associated with childhood wheeze.'

As for other allergies such as hay fever, A. C. Frosh's 1999 research came to the conclusion that 'feather pillow use . . . appears unlikely to increase the risk of developing perennial or seasonal rhinitis [all-year-round sneezing or hay fever]. In fact, in contrast with currently held views, there is evidence that the use of non-feather pillows may increase the risk.'

It would seem that the denser weave of fabrics on feather bedding (designed to keep the feathers in) also prevents dust mites from setting up home in the pillows.

Caroline Moye from Asthma UK states that 'although some people are allergic to feathers, there is no conclusive evidence to show that synthetic "hypo-allergenic" pillows are any better than synthetic ones.'

10

Greeks and Romans

Gaius Julius Caesar was born by Caesarean section

This belief is claimed to date back to Roman statesman and natural historian Pliny the Elder, who claimed that the first child to be named 'Caesar' was so-called because 'hee was ript out of his mothers bellie,' but numerous modern sources have proved this to be false.

In *Caesarean Section*, Dr Michele Moore states that 'before anaesthetics and antibiotics, C-sections were done only to deliver babies from dead mothers,' while Dr Helen Churchill, Senior Lecturer in Health Studies and Sociology, explains in *Caesarean Birth: Experience, Practice and History* that 'the association of the caesarean operation with Julius Caesar is likely to be a myth,' since there were 'no recorded maternal survivals following caesarean birth at that time (100–44 BCE) and Julius Caesar's mother lived on long after his birth'. Writing in *The Caesarean*, obstetrician Dr Michel Odent makes the point that this type of operation 'did not derive its name from the fact that Julius Caesar was born in this manner', since 'his mother, Aurelia, lived to be an adviser to her grown son'. Thus Pliny is often blamed for getting it wrong.

So how did the procedure get its name? *Caesus* is Latin for 'cut', and in *Current Obstetric and Gynaecological Diagnosis and Treatment* Dr Alan De Cherney suggests that the term probably comes from an ancient Roman decree, *lex caesarea*, which is a law that stated 'before burial of any women dying in late pregnancy the child be removed from the uterus'.

Moore suggests an alternative theory behind the origin of the term along similar lines: 'An ancestor of Caesar's was probably delivered of a dead mother . . . and the name was passed down the family.' Odent partially agrees, stating the possibility that 'an ancestor of Caesar was named after surviving the surgical birth, and the name was passed down in the family.' *Chamber's Dictionary* backs up these two theories, suggesting that the term derives from 'the Latin "to cut"' and 'from the tradition that the first bearer of the cognomen [Roman name] Caesar was delivered this way'.

So Pliny's theory that 'the first' Caesar – not Gaius Julius Caesar – was probably born this way may be true after all. If so, Julius Caesar got his name from the operation, not vice versa.

Amazons had one breast cut off so as not to hinder archery

Classical-civilization lecturer and author of *Women in Classical Athens* Susan Blundell explains that the ancient Amazon warrior women were 'reputed to have lived . . . on the south-eastern shore of the Black Sea', which clearly indicates that they were not Greek in origin.

Though Amazons are famed for removing their right breasts to stop them from impeding their fighting abilities during battles, Blundell also points out that 'no author of the classical period mentions this aspect of their appearance . . . In vase-paintings and sculptures Amazons are always shown with the normal two breasts.'

In *War and Gender*, Professor Joshua S. Goldstein describes how it was supposedly the case that Amazon women cut off one breast to make shooting a bow and arrow easier, but that 'most artistic renditions do not show this.' Lyn Webster Wilde, author of *On the Trail of the Women Warriors*, confirms that despite the stories about them 'they are always shown in art with two breasts, which are usually firm and prominent.'

So how did the myth originate?

In *Warrior Women,* archaeologist Jeannine Davis-Kimball points out that fifth-century BCE historian Herodotus 'insisted that the word Amazon stemmed from two Greek words meaning "without a breast" (*a* = without; *mazos* = breast)'. Amazon has since been given various meanings from different languages: from 'ha-mazan' meaning 'fighting together' to 'am-azon' meaning 'mother-lord'. Ancient author Philostratus suggested that 'without breast' may have meant 'not breast-fed', from the practice of military horsewomen feeding their babies mare's milk instead of breast milk. However, Blundell cautions that there is no evidence that these mastected women warriors 'ever existed', in which case the origin of the name will probably remain a mystery.

As for cutting off a breast to facilitate archery, modern women seem to cope with everyday living (and, indeed, the sport of archery) without their breasts getting in the way; surely Amazon women would have done the same?

Caligula promoted his horse to consul

The Roman Emperor Caligula was, by all accounts, not a pleasant individual, but he was very fond of his horse, Incitatus. So attached was he to the beast that rumours abounded about the animal's unlikely elevation to the position of consul.

About seventy years after Caligula's death, Roman historian Suetonius described the extent of the Emperor's affection for his trusty steed:

Besides a stall of marble, a manger of ivory, purple blankets and a collar of precious stones, he even gave this horse a house, a troop of slaves and furniture, for the more elegant entertainment of the guests invited in his name; and it is also said that he planned to make him consul.

The fact that Suetonius used 'characteristic anecdote' without giving adequate research into its authenticity means that the truth behind the rumour is debatable.

Anthony Blond, author of *A Scandalous History of the Roman Emperors*, reveals that 'making his horse into a consul never happened' and was merely a joke. The *Encyclopaedia Britannica* explains that the belief that Caligula promoted his horse to the position of consul is 'untrue'. Though it is possible that Caligula may have suggested the advancement as a joke to annoy his senators, the reality is that it never actually happened.

Atlas holds the earth on his shoulders

In the *Encyclopaedia Britannica* it is revealed that according to the Greek poet Hesiod, Atlas the Titan was punished by Zeus for waging war against him. Ancient artists consequently portrayed Atlas supporting the 'celestial globe', since this was his punishment.

In *Thereby Hangs a Tale*, lexicographer Charles E. Funk explains that the sixteenth-century Flemish map-maker Gerardus Mercator used 'a copy of one of these pictures ... as a frontispiece to his first collection of maps', which he called an 'atlas'. The name stuck as the description for a book of maps. From this, one would

Clear off, Zeus!

assume that the globe Atlas was supporting was the world, but one would be wrong.

According to the *Encyclopaedia Britannica*, 'in the works of Homer, Atlas seems to have been a marine creation who supported the pillars that held heaven and earth apart.' Classical scholars have confirmed this – Ovid: 'My grandsire Atlas holds up the skies'; Seneca: 'Atlas holds up the sky'; Horace: 'Where Atlas holds up the sky upon his shoulders.'

The key word here is 'celestial' – Atlas supported the heavens, not the earth. Did Mercator get it wrong? Possibly not. In *Mercator: The Man Who Mapped the Planet*, geographer Nicholas Crane quotes Mercator as choosing the name not because Atlas supported the world, but because he was 'so notable for his erudition, humaneness, and wisdom'.

Classical sculptures were finished in white stone or marble

According to the findings of the Museum of Classical Archaeology in Cambridge, 'Ancient Greek marble sculptures were painted in bright colours and adorned with metal jewellery.' As Peter Stewart, a lecturer in classical art reveals in his book *Statues in Roman Society*, 'statues themselves were painted roughly to resemble reality.'

Ancient chroniclers Plutarch, Virgil and Plato also made reference to painted statues, and in the 1800s, excavations on the Acropolis unearthed statues with traces of coloured paint on them.

So why do we all assume ancient statues were originally displayed in stone or marble? Possibly because eminent eighteenth-century archaeologist and art historian Johann

Joachim Winckelmann was of the strong opinion that 'colour should have a minor part in the consideration of beauty, because it is not [colour] but the structure that constitutes its essence.' Since then, nobody dared suggest that classical statues could be improved by slapping on a bit of paint.

The Museum of Classical Archaeology displays a replica of the Peplos Kore statue as it would have originally appeared, painted in blue and red, but its historical authenticity doesn't go down well with everyone: a comment in the Visitors' Book reads: 'Didn't like the Painted Woman.'

You can see images of ancient statues as they were originally intended to be seen at the website of the Virtual Sculpture Gallery and decide for yourself: http://mandarb.net/virtual_gallery/index.shtml.

Queen Cleopatra was an Egyptian

The *Encyclopaedia Britannica* reveals that although Cleopatra VII Thea Philopator was classed as an 'Egyptian queen', she was of 'Macedonian descent and had no Egyptian blood', which suggests that Queen Cleopatra was of Greek origin. Historical biographer Polly Schoyer Brooks confirms that 'though Queen of Egypt, Cleopatra was a Greek and had not one drop of Egyptian blood.' Writing in *Cleopatra*, Ernle Bradford states that 'She was the seventh Egyptian queen of her name, but it is doubtful if she had any Egyptian blood in her veins. She was a Macedonian Greek.'

If we conjure up a mental image of the great Egyptian queen she probably has long black hair and dark eye make-up. However, Bradford makes the point: 'Of her appearance we know little except from coins and descriptions in ancient writers, for no portrait busts can be fully authenticated.' He also states that neither coins nor the writers prove whether Cleopatra was blonde or brunette, fair-skinned or dark, but he does reveal that the coins do hint at an Eastern Mediterranean type, and so in his view 'it would be reasonable to infer that Cleopatra was dark haired with a pale olive skin.'

Children's historical writer Kristiana Gregory thinks otherwise, though, as her research shows that others have suggested that Cleopatra's Macedonian ancestry 'made her light-skinned, possibly with blonde hair and green eyes'. In *Ghosts of Vesuvius*, Charles Pellegrino has gone so far as to propose that she had 'fiery red hair'.

Though we may never know for sure what Queen Cleopatra's natural colouring was, it's certainly true to say she wasn't Egyptian, but rather of Macedonian Greek descent.

In gladiatorial arenas, death was indicated by a thumbs-down and a reprieve by a thumbs-up

Everyone recognizes the thumbs-down action as 'bad' or negative, and the thumbs-up gesture as 'good', but these well-known signals didn't have the same attributions in the Roman era.

It's true that the Romans used hand gestures to indicate their wishes in the gladiatorial arena: Roman satirist Juvenal records gladiators winning applause 'by slaying whoever the mob, with a turn of the thumb [*verso pollice*], bids them slay'. The poet Prudentius makes a similar observation, but neither he nor Juvenal says which way the thumb was turned.

Lexicographer Charles E. Funk suggests that the painting *Pollice Verso* by nineteenth-century French artist Jean Léon Gérôme may be responsible for 'the present popular concept that "pollice verso" meant "thumbs down".' The painting depicts a crowded Roman gladiatorial arena with some bloodthirsty vestal virgins looking down on to the final stages of combat, making downward stabbing thrusts with their thumbs. Funk goes on to explain that 'with thumb turned' may have been referring to the thumb as if it were 'a dagger pointing at oneself or thrusting into an opponent'. Funk likens the gesture to when we hitch a ride, 'by pointing the thumb in the direction we wish to travel'. In other words, the Roman 'let him have it' signal may have been more similar to the 'give us a lift' sign.

Nancy Armstrong and Melissa Wagner, authors of the *Field Guide to Gestures*, have revealed new research which suggests that 'the Romans actually hid their thumbs to spare the gladiator, displaying a closed fist, and showed their thumbs to have him slain, producing a thumb-out.' Classics expert Eric Nelson agrees, explaining that 'where we use the thumbs-up sign to signal "good job" or "yes", the Roman thumbs-up probably signified *Jugula!* ("Cut his throat!").'

Nero fiddled while Rome burned

First-century Roman Emperor Nero is traditionally blamed for setting fire to Rome in 64 AD so that he could cut through the red tape and rebuild the city to his liking. However, it would have been tricky for Nero to fiddle while the city burned as the instrument hadn't even been invented.

It's often explained that the fiddle in question was actually a lyre, and indeed second-century Roman chronicler Cassius Dio records that Nero 'climbed on to the palace roof, from which there was the best general view of the greater part of the conflagration, and assuming the lyre-player's garb, he sang the "Capture of Troy".' This account may owe something to an earlier tale written by first-century Roman chronicler Tacitus, that 'a rumour had gone forth everywhere that, at the very time when the city was in flames, the Emperor appeared on a private stage and sang of the destruction of Troy.' Indeed, Tacitus's statement is often cited as affirming Nero's guilt. However, earlier in his account he describes the cause of the blaze as 'uncertain'. He also reveals that at the start of the blaze 'Nero was at Antium' and describes how, when the Emperor returned to Rome, he had emergency shelters constructed, shipped in food and cut the price of corn to a quarter of a sesterce a pound to help the homeless. However, 'these measures, for all their popular character, earned no gratitude' due to the rumour he then goes on to repeat.

Indeed it is recorded in the *Encyclopaedia Britannica* that, during the fire, Nero was at his villa at Antium, thirty-five miles from Rome, and therefore could not be held responsible for the burning of the city.

Ancient history expert H. H. Scullard states that 'Neither charge [arson or dancing about while the fire raged] can be taken seriously: if he [Nero] had wished to destroy Rome, he would hardly have chosen a bright moonlit summer night when the movement of his fire-raisers would have been hard to hide.' Writing in *From the*

Gracchi to Nero, Scullard confirms that Nero hurried back to Rome from Antium, and 'helped to direct the firefighting and undertook energetic measures to relieve the homeless'.

Instead of being grateful for Nero's hasty endeavours to improve the city after the fire, however, the people of Rome became suspicious of his true motives, and rumours against him began to spread. Renowned for the murder of his mother, Agrippina, and his wife, Octavia, Nero found that his brutal reputation preceded him, with the result that his efforts, however well-intentioned, were rejected by his sceptical subjects.

11

Events from History

Droit du seigneur was a lord's right to spend the night with the bride of a vassal

D*roit du seigneur* or 'right of the lord', also known as *droit de cuissage* was, as the *Encyclopaedia Britannica* reveals, 'said to have existed in medieval Europe'. It is first mentioned in sixteenth-century literature (and also features in the film *Braveheart)* and is said to have originated from *jus primae noctis* or 'law of the first night'.

However, in *The Lord's First Night,* author Alain Boureau claims that the right never existed in medieval France: 'Every time we inquire into the precise context of a case . . . we find . . . no sign that these . . . statements had ever been challenged or prompted the least interaction in law or fact.'

Nineteenth-century German historian Karl Schmidt, in an 1881 treatise on the subject, concluded that it was a 'learned superstition'. According to historian Elizabeth Abbott in *A History of Celibacy*, it was rather the case that early Christian Fathers (priests) advised newlyweds to 'celebrate with chastity . . . the first night for sure and if possible the following three or four as well'. The couple could choose to decline the advice, but they were obliged

to pay a fee to the Church. Equally, feudal lords sometimes made a charge to the bridegroom for allowing him to consummate his marriage, which Abbott believes is 'probably where the myth of *jus primae noctis* and later the *droit du seigneur* originated'. Some people will tax anything . . .

At the storming of the Bastille, hundreds of prisoners were freed

The storming of the Bastille (or more correctly the Chastel Saint-Antoine) on 14 July 1789 symbolizes the beginning of the French Revolution, but the actual number of prisoners released on that day is far fewer than most people realize: there were only seven people confined in the building at the time.

Four were criminally convicted note-forgers and two were mentally unstable, one of whom, Jean-Baptiste Tavernier had been placed in the Bastille at his family's behest because the prison was more comfortable than the asylum.

The seventh resident, who had also been placed in the Bastille at the request of his family, was the Count de Solages. A friend of the Marquis de Sade, the Count had been locked up for 'atrocious crimes for which life imprisonment was not too harsh', according to Guy Chaussinand-Nogaret, French historian and author of *The French Nobility in the Eighteenth Century*.

After the storming, the four forgers were rearrested and reincarcerated, and both lunatics were promptly returned to the Charenton asylum. Only the Count de Solages retained his freedom. According to historian Simon Schama in *Citizens*: 'He was given free lodgings at the Hôtel de Rouen ... before disappearing into the city, much to the regret of his relatives.'

Gondolas are painted black because they carried victims of the Black Death

The Black Death ravaged Europe between 1347 and 1351, but according to the *Encyclopaedia Britannica*, it wasn't for another 200 years that the formerly 'colourful and lavishly decorated' Venetian gondolas began to be painted black. As far as the Institute for the Conservation of Gondolas and the Tutoring of Gondoliers is concerned, the 'legends that attribute it [the black-painted hull] to the commemoration of the plague are considered groundless'. So what is the real reason for the change in the colour of these vessels?

Apparently it was due to a 'sumptuary' [expenditure-limiting] law being passed to regulate their appearance. In the seventeenth century, Venetian nobles would compete with each other over who had the most brightly painted gondola. The ornamentation on these gondolas must have become upsettingly ostentatious because, according to gondola maker Thom Price, to put a stop to all the showing-off 'the Doge handed down a decree . . . requiring that all gondolas be painted black.' The only gondolas that were exempt from this rule were those belonging to dignitaries.

The Institute goes on to describe how the 'black colour (on the hull) . . . is a characteristic of all Venetian boats, and it is due to the use of pitch as a waterproofing agent'. Price agrees, explaining that a gondola 'used to be sealed with pitch to keep it watertight, and since the pitch is black, it was easiest to paint the boat black'.

In the Wild West, six-shooters shot six bullets

While watching Westerns, my dad likes to count the number of bullets released, to check that none of the gunslingers fires more than six in a row. However, it would appear that Wild West professional gunmen would only have ever fired a maximum of five bullets before reloading.

Wild West lawman Wyatt Earp, who was involved in the Gunfight at the O.K. Corral, and who was interviewed in 1928 by a contemporary, Stuart N. Lake, explains why:

> I have often been asked why five shots without reloading were all a top-notch gunfighter fired, when his guns were chambered for six cartridges. The answer is, merely, safety. To ensure against accidental discharge of the gun while in the holster, due to hair-trigger adjustment, the hammer rested upon an empty chamber.

In other words, the fact that these guns had no safety catches meant that if a gun contained six bullets, the merest knock to the hammer could cause the gun to fire a bullet while in its holster. Hence the expression to shoot one's self in the foot.

Popular Mechanics writer Cliff Gromer confirms that because original six-guns had no safety catch, it was necessary to load just five rounds into the cylinder and carry the gun with the hammer down over the empty chamber. This way, 'there was no way the gun could go off without first cocking the hammer', and so accidental misfires could be more easily prevented. He adds intriguingly that 'gunslingers in the Old West used to take advantage of the empty chamber by stuffing it with a rolled-up five-dollar bill. That way, if they came out second best in a duel, the dough could be used for a decent burial.'

The *Titanic* was described by her owners as 'unsinkable'

The ill-fated liner is famed for being optimistically described by her owners as 'unsinkable', but was she really so described?

Practically, I said, practically unsinkable.

In *The Titanic*, Michael Davie refers to the content of Sir Philip Gibbs's 1912 oddly titled pamphlet *The Deathless Story of the Titanic,* which quotes the owners describing the watertight-bulkhead arrangement on the vessel as 'practically making the ship unsinkable'. Furthermore, historian Daniel Allen Butler, the author of *Unsinkable*, points out that in 'the prestigious British journal *Shipbuilder* . . . the authors . . . labelled the ships *practically* unsinkable'. The word 'practically' appears to have been edited out of subsequent promotional literature about the *Titanic*.

This example serves as a lesson to all pedantic grammarians that, on occasions, qualifiers should be allowed to remain.

The *Mary Celeste* was found abandoned in mysterious circumstances

In 1872, the *Mary Celeste* was discovered off the coast of Gibraltar. Full mugs of tea and half-eaten breakfasts were allegedly found, but where was the crew? Had they been attacked by pirates, abducted by aliens, eaten by a giant squid or simply disappeared into thin air? The British officials who heard the case ruled out foul play and merely moved on to their next case: the derelict vessel, *The Latin*. In the nineteenth century, ships' crews often went missing and nobody thought too much about it.

The public's fascination with the *Mary Celeste* (author of *Seafaring Lore and Legend* Peter D. Jeans points out that official documents stated that 'the vessel's name was *Mary Celeste*') dates back to Arthur Conan Doyle's 1883 anonymous fictionalized account of the tale, 'J. Habakkuk

Jepson's Statement'. It is here that Doyle alters the vessel's name from *Mary Celeste* to *Marie Celeste*. In Doyle's version the ship is commandeered, sailed to Africa and the passengers and crew are murdered. In *After the Storm*, maritime author John Rousmaniere quotes Doyle as saying: 'When I wrote a yarn round the incident . . . it was done irresponsibly and I never imagined it would be seriously analysed.'

When the *Mary Celeste* was discovered, Jeans explains that according to eyewitness statements they found 'her only boat gone' and there was 'a frayed . . . painter [mooring rope] hanging over the stern'. He also refers to the fact that 'the ship's sextant, chronometer, and register were also missing.'

Barring the notion of a giant squid with an ability to gnaw through rope and a taste for sailing instruments, the captain, his wife and daughter and crew of seven had clearly abandoned ship – possibly fearing their cargo of alcohol was about to explode. It then appears that they became separated from their vessel and most likely perished at sea. Not so mysterious after all then.

'Ring-a-ring-o'roses' is a nursery rhyme about the Great Plague

Editors of *The Oxford Dictionary of Nursery Rhymes*, Iona and Peter Opie, have come to the conclusion that in the modern English versions of the rhyme the references to sneezing and falling down have led to would-be origin finders claiming that it dates back to the days of the Great Plague. 'A rosy rash,' the Opies allege, 'was a symptom of the plague, posies of herbs were carried as protection, sneezing was a final fatal symptom, and "all fall down" was exactly what happened.' But the Opies point out that the earliest rhyme of this style – 'Ring a ring of rosie / A bottle full of posie / All the girls in our town / Ring for little Josie' – was sung around 1790, and clearly makes no mention of pustulating sores.

Indeed, the US-based Center for Disease Control and Prevention reveals that the main symptom of bubonic plague is a swelling or 'bubo' as well as 'fever, chills, cough, and breathing difficulty', and makes no mention of rashes or sneezing.

The 'All fall down' version wasn't noted down until 1881, and since the Great Plague happened in 1665, that would mean the rhyme would have to have been handed down orally for more than two hundred years, or five hundred years if it refers to the Black Death of 1348. According to the Opies, by 1898 there were 'twelve versions', in most of which 'the "A-tishoo" was notably absent'. They suggest that the rose petal reference could be associated with the 'old belief that gifted children had the power to laugh roses', and also add that 'the foreign nineteenth-century versions seem to show that the fall was originally a curtsy or other gracious movement.'

Nursery-rhyme researcher and author of *Mother Goose: From Nursery to Literature* Gloria T. Delamar points out that 'the time-lapse between the plague and the appearance of the game, diminishes ... [the plague] theory.' She suspects that the plague connection will continue to be made, 'probably because people, in some perverse way, would like to believe that the innocent rhyme has a grim history'.

Personally, I've always thought of the original rhyme as a warning against the scourges of hay fever ...

Militant activity by suffragettes won votes for women

In 1903, Emmeline Pankhurst founded the Women's Social and Political Union. The suffragette movement grew more militant during the following eleven years, but made little headway, possibly because, according to suffragist, Millicent Garrett Fawcett, its 'greatest enemy was the Prime Minister, Mr Asquith'. In fact, according to historian Sean Lang, by 1914 'all the efforts of the suffragettes had failed. The government was set against votes for women, and that was that.'

At the start of the First World War, woman-suffrage organizations began to focus their energies on the war effort rather than headline-making militancy, and according to the *Encyclopaedia Britannica*, 'their effectiveness did much to win the public wholeheartedly to the cause of woman suffrage' to the extent that by 1915, even Asquith seems to have been won round. In *Suffragettes and Votes for Women*, historian L. E. Snellgrove quotes him as saying: 'When the war comes to an end . . . have not the women a special claim to be heard . . . I cannot deny that claim.'

History professor Nicoletta F. Gullace points out in *The Blood of Our Sons* that 'Asquith attributed his "conversion" to women's suffrage to the heroic actions of women like Edith Cavell, who had "taught the bravest man amongst us a supreme lesson of courage".' (Giving one's life for one's country certainly appears braver than the 1914 hatchet attack launched on National Gallery artworks by suffragette, Mary Richardson.)

In 1928, twenty-five years after the suffragettes began

their campaign, all women over the age of twenty-one were finally given the vote. Historian and author of *Modern Britain* John L. Irwin concludes that 'the involvement of women in war work of various kinds did more for their cause than the demonstrations against the government.'

History may not portray women war workers as charismatically as suffragettes, but surely they are the real heroines of women's suffrage.

The Great Plague of 1665 was halted by the Great Fire of London in 1666

The *Encyclopaedia Britannica* informs us that 'the disappearance of plague from London has been attributed to the Great Fire in September 1666, but it also subsided in other cities without such cause.'

A BAD DAY IN 1666

Your house is on fire!

I'm afraid you've got the plague.

University of London historian Dr Justin Champion confirms that the geography of the disease and the location of the fire have no correlation with regard to the halting of the plague, as 'most of the deaths were in the poor suburban parishes east, north and south of the City walls,' a considerable distance from where the fire was raging.

Simon Thurley, director of the Museum of London, is in full agreement: 'The Great Fire of 1666 could not be responsible [for ending the Great Plague] since it was almost totally confined to the City, and even there, the parishes most affected by plague (to the north and east) were untouched by the fire.'

What did cause the disappearance of the plague in London after 1665 is still a great mystery. Champion suggests that 'mutation of the bacteria, improvements in diet and health, the changing built environment may all have had a role,' while *Britannica* concludes that 'the cessation of plague in England must be regarded as spontaneous.'

One thing is certain: the Great Fire of London does not appear to deserve the credit it has formally taken.

The *Hindenburg* exploded due to hydrogen combustion

On 6 May 1937 the German zeppelin *Hindenburg* burned up when attempting to dock at Lakehurst Naval Air Station, New Jersey, USA.

Prior to the disaster, zeppelins had had an excellent safety record, and according to the *Encyclopaedia Britannica* they could make flights of almost one hundred hours' duration.

In a contemporary article written by a *Manchester Guardian* correspondent, it was revealed that 'the bar and smoking room had nine panels illustrating previous lighter-than-air vessels, one showing the first Zeppelin of 1900.' Strange though it may seem, it really did have a smoking room, and after the disaster, the world mocked the foolhardiness of the zeppelin's designers for using explosive hydrogen to lift the airship. This ridicule, however, may have been misplaced.

NASA scientist Addison Bain and physicist Ulrich Schmidtchen have drawn attention to archived letters written by electrical engineer Otto Beyersdorff at the time of the investigation, which stated: 'The actual cause of the fire was the extremely easy flammability of the covering material brought about by the discharges of an electrostatic nature.'

This evidence has led Bain and Schmidtchen to believe that the disaster had nothing to do with the presence of hydrogen gas on board the airship. They claim that the chief cause was 'the chemical and electrical properties of the paint of the outer shell in connection with the particular meteorological conditions prevailing in Lakehurst on the day of the accident'.

Chemist and author of *Chemistry Demystified* Linda Williams agrees: 'Static electricity had set fire to the aluminium-rich varnish of the airship's fabric covering, [and] ignited the hydrogen within.'

Bain and Schmidtchen point out that alongside other gases, such as natural gas or propane, hydrogen is not known for being more problematic, and therefore 'neither are the risks associated with it any greater'. So the designers of the ill-fated *Hindenburg* hadn't been so foolish in their choice of lifting agent, but the fact that they had painted it with what amounted to rocket fuel means they don't come away completely blameless.

Although the disaster looked horrific, around two-thirds of the passengers and crew survived the ordeal, many by jumping through windows as the ship neared the ground. Captain Ernst Lehmann was led away from the crash muttering, 'I can't understand it.' He died the next day.

12

Questionable Quotes

During a speech in Berlin in 1963, John F. Kennedy called himself 'a doughnut'

In one of his last *Letters from America* programmes broadcast on BBC Radio Four, the late, great Alistair Cook recalled the tale of Kennedy's alleged goof most eloquently:

> I watched this immensely moving scene on television and was, like millions more I imagine, startled by the strange noise that came up from the crowd. It was an immediate, huge peal of laughter, modulating in about two seconds, into a roaring ocean of applause ... What John F. Kennedy had proclaimed with such courage and determination was: 'I am a jelly doughnut – Ich bin ein Berliner!'

In the German language, it is generally the case that the indefinite article (*ein*) is omitted in sentences describing where people are from, and so this led to claims that what Kennedy should have said was 'Ich bin Berliner'. But was he claiming to hail from Berlin? According to German linguistics professor Jürgen Eichhoff, '"Ich bin ein Berliner" is ... the one and only correct way of expressing in German what the President intended to say,' which was not 'I hail from

Berlin' (because with his strong American accent it was clear that he didn't), but rather 'I stand with the people of Berlin.'

And is *ein Berliner* a type of 'jelly doughnut'? Eichhoff reveals that outside the city of Berlin, a Berliner is indeed a variety of doughnut, but within Berlin, the pastry is termed a *Pfannkuchen*. Technically speaking, it is possible to translate the phrase 'Ich bin ein Berliner' as 'I am a doughnut,' but this would be similar to assuming that people who stated they came from Wales had just left the company of some large sea mammals. In Eichhoff's view 'there is not the slightest chance that anyone in the audience could have interpreted "Berliner" as denoting a jelly-filled doughnut.'

But what about the delayed laughter remarked upon by Alistair Cook? The likely reason for this was that Kennedy made a joke which was only audible to his audience. After his interpreter had felt the need to translate 'Ich bin ein Berliner' into German, Kennedy paused for a moment and quipped: 'I appreciate my interpreter translating my German.' It was this remark that provoked the laughter. The President then ended his speech with a reworking of the Berliner phrase: 'And, therefore, as a free man, I take pride in the words "Ich bin ein Berliner".'

There was no embarrassed silence: the crowd's cheers and applause were immediate. The myth may have originated from an article in the *New York Times* in April 1988, entitled 'I Am a Jelly-Filled Doughnut', which claimed that the crowd had giggled at the phrase rather than the joke.

You can decide for yourself if you think the crowd laughed at his words by listening to the speech at: www.americanrhetoric.com/speeches/jfkichbineinberliner. html.

Marie Antoinette said 'Let them eat cake'

In book VI of *The Confessions of Jean-Jacques Rousseau,* written in 1736, the French philosopher stated: 'I recollected the thoughtless saying of a great princess, who, on being informed that the country people had no bread, replied, "Then let them eat pastry!"' Rousseau did not mention Marie Antoinette by name. This may have been because, in 1736, Marie Antoinette was minus nineteen years old, which rather rules her out as the originator of the phrase.

Besides, according to historian Lady Antonia Fraser, the statement was 'callous and ignorant', and Marie Antoinette 'was neither'. In her biography, *Marie Antoinette*, Fraser claims that the phrase was uttered 'a hundred years before her by Marie Thérèse, the wife of Louis XIV'.

It would also seem that the phrase 'Qu'ils mangent de la brioche', which is generally translated as 'Let them eat cake,' has achieved more notoriety than it deserves. Author of *The Oxford Companion to Food* Alan Davidson explains that 'eighteenth-century brioche was only lightly enriched (by modest quantities of butter and eggs) and not very far removed from a good white loaf of bread.'

Charles Darwin originated the phrase 'Survival of the fittest'

Though Darwin is closely associated with the phrase 'survival of the fittest', these words never appeared in any of his work. In fact, the real originator of the expression was Herbert Spencer, a nineteenth-century English sociologist and philosopher who was, as the *Encyclopaedia*

Britannica reveals, 'an early advocate of the theory of evolution'.

According to politics professor David Weinstein in *Equal Freedom and Utility*, Spencer claimed that 'he was the first to use the expression "survival of the fittest".' Indeed, the words were first printed in Spencer's *Principles of Biology* in 1864, five years after Darwin's *On the Origin of Species* was published.

'Music hath charms to soothe the savage beast'

This misquote, often attributed to William Shakespeare, comes from seventeenth-century English dramatist William Congreve's play *The Mourning Bride* (Act I,

It's not often that you see such a fine illustration of the dangers of misquoting.

Scene 1). The correct quote runs: 'Music hath charms to soothe the savage breast, / To soften rocks, or bend a knotted oak.'

Greta Garbo never said 'I want to be alone'

In her 1990 autobiography, *Garbo: Her Story*, Greta Garbo insisted she only ever said: 'I want to be left alone.' However, according to the *Encyclopaedia Britannica*, it was in the 1932 film *Grand Hotel* that 'she first uttered her signature line of "I want to be alone"'.

A viewing of the film confirms that Garbo does indeed speak the phrase quite clearly, and not just once, but on three occasions. In the role of a Russian woman named Grusinskaya, the first utterance comes after thirty-four minutes:

> Theatre manager: Who is she? Where does she think she is? Russia? Well?
> Grusinskaya: I want to be alone.
> Theatre manager: Where have you been? I suppose I can cancel the Vienna contract?
> Grusinskaya: I just want to be alone.

And then again after forty minutes:

> Baron: I'm not going. You know I'm not going. Oh, please let me stay.
> Grusinskaya: But I want to be alone.

Interestingly, even though Swedish-born Garbo was playing a Russian character, she doesn't pronounce 'want' as 'vont' as her imitators often suggest. She pronounces the 'w' quite distinctly in the correct English fashion.

When Garbo denied ever saying the phrase, claiming only to have said, '"I want to be left alone," there is a whole world of difference,' perhaps she was making a comment on her private life rather than a literal reference to her on-screen scripted quotes.

James Cagney said 'You dirty rat!'

The *Encyclopaedia Britannica* reveals that: 'Contrary to the popular perception created by scores of impressionists throughout the years, Cagney neither said "You dirty rat!" nor "All right, you guys!" in any film.'

According to biographer John McCabe in his book *Cagney*, the closest the actor came to uttering these words was in the 1932 film *Taxi!*, when he shouted, 'Come out and take it, you dirty, yellow-bellied rat, or I'll give it to you through the door!'

Sherlock Holmes said 'Elementary, my dear Watson'

Sherlock Holmes's famous line doesn't appear in any of the Sherlock Holmes chronicles written by Arthur Conan Doyle. In fact Holmes only ever said, 'Elementary.'

According to the findings of www.saidwhat.co.uk, the phrase 'Elementary, my dear Watson' first appeared in a film review featured in the *New York Times* on 19 October 1929.

As a point of interest, Holmes is never described as sporting a deerstalker hat in the novels, despite its prevalence in the many film versions. The headgear was added by the illustrator Sidney Paget, when producing drawings for the *Strand Magazine*.

"Tis better to have loved and lost, than never to have loved at all' refers to romantic love

These words come from an elegy published in 1850, *In Memoriam A. H. H.*, by nineteenth-century English poet and dramatist Alfred Tennyson. However, A. H. H. was not a woman, but a fellow student, essayist and poet, Arthur Henry Hallam, whom Tennyson met at Trinity College, Cambridge.

The *Encyclopaedia Britannica* describes this friendship as 'the deepest friendship of Tennyson's life'. Hallam had been due to marry Tennyson's sister, Emily, but he died suddenly at the age of twenty-two.

Nor was Tennyson the first to come up with this moving sentiment. One hundred and fifty years earlier, English dramatist William Congreve, in his 1700 play *The Way of the World*, wrote: ''Tis better to be left than never to have lov'd.'

Did you know . . . ?

Although it is well known that, 'A little knowledge is a dangerous thing', in his 1711 *An Essay on Criticism*, what English poet and satirist Alexander Pope actually said was: 'A little learning is a dangerous thing.'

13

Historical Figures

Anna Leonowens was a governess of renown in the court of Siam

In the preface to Anna Leonowens's 1870 book *The English Governess at the Siamese Court* it is written: 'In 1851, Anna married a young British officer named Thomas Leonowens.' William Warren, author of the commentary *Who Was Anna Leonowens?*, points out that she had actually married 'a lowly . . . clerk, whose name was not Leonowens, but Thomas Leon Owens'.

The title of Leonowens's book purports to describe her given role in the court, but Warren comments: 'King Mongkut's correspondence makes clear, she [Anna] was not hired as a governess . . . but merely as a teacher of English.' An excerpt from one of the King's letters confirms this: 'we hope that . . . you will do your best endeavour for knowledge of English language . . . and literature.'

In the sequel to her first book, *The Romance of the Harem*, Leonowens describes how King Mongkut threw out-of-favour wives into underground dungeons below the Grand Palace, and claims to have witnessed the public torture and burning of the consort Tuptim and a priest she had fallen in love with. However, according to William Warren:

> There were no underground dungeons at the Grand Palace or anywhere else in Bangkok . . . there could not have been in that watery soil . . . Nor was there any public burning, or, if there was, it escaped the attention of every other foreign resident, many of whom also wrote accounts of the same period.

In *Anna Leonowens: A Life Beyond 'The King and I'*, biographer Leslie Smith Dow describes a meeting between Anna and King Chulalongkorn, King Mongkut's son, in London in 1897 recounted by her granddaughter:

> The King looked intently at her grandmother, and remarked, 'Mem, why did you write such a wicked book about my father King Mongkut? You know that you have made him utterly ridiculous and now the whole world laughs at your descriptions of him and at his memory. Oh, why, how could you do it?'

Dr W. S. Bristowe was the first academic to question Leonowens's account of her stay in Siam (modern-day Thailand). While researching a book on her son Louis, the academic found several discrepancies in her story. He has suggested that the inventions and distortions in Leonowens's books may have been partly designed to boost sales. Warren agrees, and has suggested that when writing her sequel: 'Anna simply invented such tales, perhaps to add some spice.'

Abraham Lincoln was an abolitionist

While it is true that in 1840s America there were people who believed that slavery was a shameful violation of human rights that should be abolished immediately, historian James M. McPherson reveals that Abraham Lincoln wasn't one of them.

In *Battle Cry of Freedom*, McPherson quotes Lincoln as saying that '"the promulgation of abolition doctrines tends rather to increase than to abate its evils" by uniting the South in defence of the institution.' Indeed, on an 1864 campaign poster printed in Henry Steele Commager's *American Civil War*, Lincoln is quoted as saying: 'My paramount object is to save the Union, and not either to save or destroy Slavery.'

Former presidential speechwriter and political lecturer James C. Humes confirms this fact in *The Wit and Wisdom of Abraham Lincoln*: 'Even when he [Lincoln] became a Republican he was no abolitionist, even though he accepted abolitionists' support.'

During a debate in 1858, Lincoln said of black slaves: 'He is not my equal in many respects – certainly not in colour, perhaps not in moral or intellectual endowments. But in the right to eat the bread, without leave of anybody else, which his own hand earns, he is my equal, and the equal of . . . every living man.'

Perhaps Lincoln believed racial integration was unfeasible in the mid-nineteenth century or, as a wily politician, he may have been presenting a 'moderate' as opposed to 'radical' position to win votes. Indeed, his 1863 Gettysburg Address echoed the 1776 Declaration of Independence with his reference to 'all men are created equal,' and in his support for the notion that 'government of the people . . . by the people . . . for the people shall not perish from this earth.'

Pulitzer Prize-winner and author of *Lincoln Reconsidered*, David Herbert Donald, came to the conclusion that while Lincoln believed that 'slavery was a moral wrong' which he was 'not sure how to right', it was also clear that the US President was certainly 'not an abolitionist'.

Benjamin Disraeli was Britain's only Jewish Prime Minister

Until the age of thirteen Benjamin Disraeli (1804–81) was Jewish. Described as being 'of Italian-Jewish descent' in the *Encyclopaedia Britannica*, it was his father's quarrel with the synagogue of Bevis Marks in 1813 that led to the decision to have Benjamin and his siblings baptized as Christians four years later, at which point the young Disraeli became an Anglican.

Until 1858 followers of the Jewish faith were excluded from Parliament, and so his father's timely decision allowed Disraeli to follow a career path that would otherwise have been closed to him, and at sixty-four, he became Prime Minister.

According to biographer Robert Blake, Disraeli was 'fascinated by the connection between Judaism and Christianity, and supposedly told Queen Victoria: "I am the blank page between the Old and New Testament."'

Technically, therefore, the honour of being Britain's first practising Jewish Prime Minister remains open.

Catherine the Great's amorous interest in horses led to her death

Biographer John T. Alexander explains that after the death of the eighteenth-century Russian empress Catherine the Great, rumours about her soon began circulating in France concerning the fact that she had 'an immense sexual appetite which was the cause of her death when a horse was lowered on her too suddenly'. (Surely she'd have spotted a whole horse bearing down on her at speed?)

No blame can be attached to me.

In *Catherine the Great*, Alexander attempts to set the record straight: 'While Catherine's sexual appetite was admittedly large, it did not require staff assistance, and it did not run to horses.' In fact, he cites a more humdrum death, explaining that at the age of sixty-seven, 'the Empress suffered an attack of apoplexy . . . while sitting on her commode, and died in her bed two days later.'

Carolly Erickson, author of *Great Catherine,* also confirms the unfortunate chain of events leading to Catherine's demise: 'the chamberlain Zotov . . . went to the water-closet that adjoined the main room. There, on the floor, was the Empress, her gown crumpled immodestly around her legs, her face blood-red and her cap awry.'

The culprits responsible for starting the rumours about the alleged horseplay were possibly French anti-monarchists. Alexander states that their aim was to undermine Catherine's claims to greatness, 'by aggressively asserting that her primary motivation was unbridled sex [literally, it would appear] – the excesses of which resulted in her monstrous death'. They were undoubtedly successful since the rumour of her equine affiliation continues to persist to this day.

Catherine was a benevolent despot, as despots go, and the time has come to clear her name once and for all.

Dick Turpin rode to York in a day on Black Bess

Legend has it that romantic eighteenth-century highway-man Dick Turpin (1705–39) rode from London to York in one day to establish an alibi for himself, but legend has it wrong. If the feat was achieved, it is not Turpin who deserves the credit. In *The Oxford Companion to British History*, author and history professor John Ashton Cannon points out that it was 'John [also known as William] Nevison, or "Swift Nick", who made the ride'.

Daniel Defoe recounts in *A Tour Through the Whole Island of Great Britain* how, in 1676 at Gads Hill, Kent: 'a gentleman was robb'd by one "Nicks" on a bay mare . . . he rode across the county of Essex . . . to York the same afternoon.' On his arrival in York, 'Nicks' took the bold step of approaching the Lord Mayor to ask him 'what o'clock it was'. Although he was arrested for the crime, in a subsequent trial the jury acquitted him of any involvement in the robbery, because he had cleverly covered his tracks by ensuring his whereabouts had been verified by an important local official.

As 'Dauntless Dick', Dick Turpin later gained credit for the exploit when Victorian novelist Harrison Ainsworth attributed Nevison's feat to Turpin in his 1834 romance *Rookwood*. According to Gordon Maxwell, author of *Highwayman's Heath*: 'in addition to giving Dick Turpin a fame that did not belong to him, he [Ainsworth] also tried to steal more thunder for his hero, who was the "Flying Highwayman" [Nevison], not Turpin.' So popular was the romantic fiction that the story soon eclipsed the tales of the criminal's real activities. Turpin's gallantry was, to say the least, exaggerated: he once roasted a widow over an open fire to make her reveal the whereabouts of her savings.

With regard to the legend of Turpin's horse Black Bess, James Sharpe, author of *Dick Turpin: The Myth of the English Highwayman*, reveals that Ainsworth borrowed the image of the mythical mare from an 1825 poem that began: 'Bold Turpin upon Hounslow Heath / His black mare Bess bestrode.' She has since become part of the legend, even though she never existed.

Emily Davison threw herself under the King's horse to become a martyr

On 4 June 1913, at the Epsom Derby, suffragette Emily Davison made the ultimate sacrifice and threw herself under the hooves of Anmer, King George V's horse, or so the story goes, even though there is no evidence to prove that Davison intended to make herself a martyr. Eyewitness John Ervine reported that at the time of the incident Emily 'put up her hand, but whether it was to catch hold of the reins or to protect herself I do not know'.

A police report disclosed that the contents of Emily Davison's handbag revealed a return ticket to Epsom and a diary with appointments for the following weeks. In *Women's Lives Into Print*, contributor Liz Stanley also points out that Davison had 'a race card marked with her fancies (do suicides mark race cards and place bets thirty minutes before they die?)', and that her bag contained 'a helper's pass card to work at a Kensington suffragette bazaar which didn't open until . . . after the Derby was over'. The evidence presented at the inquest raised similarly strong doubts about the likelihood of her death being a suicide, and a verdict of 'Death by Misadventure' was returned.

Writing in *The Suffragette Movement*, fellow suffragette Sylvia Pankhurst didn't feel the act was one of suicide, and suggested that Emily had hoped simply to bring a halt to the race through the sudden act of 'a mere waving of the purple-white-and-green at Tattenham

Corner'. Furthermore, she felt strongly that Davison 'would not thus have died without writing a farewell message to her mother'.

In *The Life and Death of Emily Wilding Davison* biographers Ann Morley and Liz Stanley conclude that 'she knew she might be injured or killed, hoped she would not be, but willingly took the risk.'

Emily's return ticket can be seen at The Women's Library, Old Castle Street, London. The amateur footage of the event can be viewed at: www.firstworldwar.com/video/epsomsuffragette.htm.

Hans Brinker saved Holland by putting his finger in a leaking dyke

This fearless lad is commemorated by a statue in Spaarndam, in the Netherlands, along with an inscription that reads: 'Dedicated to our youth to honor [*sic*] the boy who symbolizes Holland's perpetual struggle against water.'

It is odd that the young man isn't named, but this is most likely because he never existed. The word 'symbolizes' was aptly chosen because the tale of Hans Brinker wasn't true and nor did it even have Dutch origins.

Nineteenth-century US author Mary Mapes Dodge portrayed the tale as a Dutch folk legend in the children's fiction book *Hans Brinker, or the Silver Skates* in 1865, in which a Dutch boy saved the region from flooding by plugging a leaking dyke with his finger and staying there all night despite a heavy storm. In fact, when Dodge wrote the novel, she hadn't ever visited the Netherlands, and it would seem that the names Hans and Gretel have been borrowed from tales by the German Brothers Grimm. *Hans Brinker, or the Silver Skates* was translated into Dutch in 1867 with the qualification: 'This sweet story is entirely the author's view.' Quite.

But why build a statue to honour a non-existent folk hero? It appears to be the case that foreign tourists who arrived at Spaarndam were often disappointed to find no dyke and no Dutch boy, and so in 1950, the Dutch Bureau for Tourism obligingly commissioned a statue. In 1954 Dutch author Margreet Bruijn rewrote the story.

As for dyke-saving, Dutch ethnologist Theo Meder explains that in the Netherlands, coastal towns are protected from the sea mainly by dunes, whereas dykes are used inland against rivers and lakes: 'When the water comes, the clay gets soaked . . . and the dykes cave in . . . a finger in the dyke won't help a bit.'

... so in the end we thought it would be easier to leave him there.

It's a credit to Mary Mapes Dodge that her work of fiction should provoke such a passionate response from her readers, but it's also clear that the actions of the Dutch Tourism Bureau have certainly helped to perpetuate this much-loved myth.

Hitler was a teetotal vegetarian

On 30 May 1937, an article in the *New York Times* stated: 'It is well known that Hitler is a vegetarian and does not drink or smoke ... His lunch and dinner consist ... of soup, eggs, vegetables and mineral water, although he occasionally relishes a slice of ham.' Vegetarian ham, perhaps?

In *The Life and Death of Adolf Hitler* biographer Robert Payne says that Hitler 'drank beer and diluted wine frequently, [and] had a special fondness for Bavarian sausages.' Beer, wine and sausages? Salvatore Paolini, a former waiter to Hitler confirms: 'On the whole, he never ate meat ... but he did like sausages and ham.' While chef Dione Lucas, who worked in a Hamburg restaurant that Hitler frequented during the late 1930s, said his favourite dish was 'stuffed squab' (young pigeon).

Hitler was clearly the poultry-eating, sausage- and ham-loving kind of vegetarian.

Nelson lost an eye, wore an eyepatch and said 'I see no ships'

In *The Nelson Encyclopedia*, historian Colin White makes the point that 'no contemporary portrait shows him [Nelson] with such a patch, and none of the many contemporary descriptions of his appearance mention it,' and explains that the fallacy probably arose because it is commonly said that Nelson 'lost' an eye. White reveals that Nelson 'lost only the sight of the eye, as the result of an internal injury, when he was hit in the face by gravel at the siege of Calvi in Corsica in July 1794 . . . there was no external sign to indicate which eye was blind.'

However, Nelson is sometimes described as protecting his good eye by wearing a patch over it. A sensible precaution on the one hand, but which, on the other, would surely have made things rather difficult to see. White explains that what Nelson wore was a 'green felt . . . eye-shade . . . to keep the glare of the sun out of his good left eye'. Artist Arthur Devis painted a posthumous portrait of Nelson wearing a hat with his eye-shade attached to the brim. It is possible to see one such hat complete with eye-shade at the Undercroft Museum at Westminster Abbey.

During the Battle of Copenhagen in 1801, Nelson chose to ignore an order from his commander-in-chief to discontinue action against the Danish fleet. He is supposed to have put his telescope to his blind eye and said, 'I see no ships,' but this would have sounded more than a little odd as he was in the middle of a sea battle. In his 1845 *Despatches and Letters of Nelson*, Colonel William Stewart explains that what Nelson actually said was: 'I really do not see the signal!' This selective blindness allowed Nelson to press on with the battle against the odds and win the day.

George Washington chopped down a cherry tree and had wooden teeth

Allen A. Metcalf writing in *Presidential Voices* is certain that George Washington never had wooden teeth. He explains that Washington's dentist John Greenwood 'made four of the six sets of false teeth Washington wore during his lifetime'. These included 'a lower plate with eight human teeth set in hippopotamus bone' followed by 'a thin gold plate holding ivory teeth at the top . . . and teeth carved from elephant ivory at the bottom.' Metcalf adds that 'false teeth never have been made of wood. The saliva in the mouth would soon turn them to mush.'

Gilbert Stuart, who painted Washington in 1796, noted that 'he just had a set of false teeth inserted, which accounts for the constrained expression so noticeable about the mouth.'

The lower set of these dentures is on display in the Dr Samuel D. Harris National Museum of Dentistry in Baltimore. Fraunces Tavern Museum in New York also includes specimens of Washington's false teeth.

As for the cherry-tree tale, the story goes that young George wanted to try out a new axe and chopped down his father's cherry tree. When questioned by his father about it, he is supposed to have uttered the famous line: 'I cannot tell a lie. It was I who chopped down the cherry tree.'

However, the *Encyclopaedia Britannica* states that the originator of the story was an American clergyman and itinerant book agent, Parson Weems: 'This fiction was inserted into the fifth edition (1806) of Weems's book *The Life and Memorable Actions of George Washington.*'

Evidently, Weems invented the tale to emphasize the importance of being truthful and honest.

John F. Kennedy could not have been killed by a lone gunman firing two shots

On 22 November 1963, President John F. Kennedy was assassinated in Dallas, Texas. Governor John B. Connally was also shot. Abraham Zapruder captured the event on film, but though Lee Harvey Oswald was arrested for the crime, he was shot dead before he could stand trial.

Since the first bullet hit only President Kennedy, few people believed that a lone gunman could have shot Kennedy again, and Connally, with the second bullet. This became known as the 'single-bullet theory'. A third bullet was said to have been fired from a grassy knoll ahead of the motorcade, implying that Oswald had an accomplice.

Computer animator Dale Myers has studied the assassination for more than twenty-five years and has devised a three-dimensional computer animation of the events. 'Talk about all the theories you want,' he has said. 'This thing happened only one way.'

Contrary to impressions given in Oliver Stone's 1991 film *JFK*, Governor Connally was sitting six inches inboard of Kennedy, and three inches lower on a jumpseat, and he turned sharply to his right. In this position, Myers argues that it is perfectly feasible for a single bullet to have hit both men, which makes it 'not a single-bullet *theory*, but a single-bullet *fact*'.

In 1979, the House Select Committee on Assassinations heard evidence from researchers stating that acoustic evidence, allegedly accidentally recorded by Dallas Police Officer H. P. McLain's radio microphone, pointed to a high probability that a shot had been fired from the grassy knoll.

Again, using computer animation, Myers refutes this: 'H. P. McLain could not have been where the acoustics evidence predicted. Therefore the acoustics evidence is invalid.' Indeed, McLain himself confirms this, stating of the acoustic recording: 'I don't care what they say. It wasn't mine.'

And as for any suggestions that Oswald was a mediocre marksman, his Marine Corps scorecards show an excellent hit rate at 200 yards, twice the distance from the book depository to Kennedy's vehicle. Author John Lattimer states that Oswald was 'not only a very good shot, but consistent'.

14

Inventions, Achievements and Discoveries

The first European to discover Australia was Captain Cook

In 1768, the Royal Society in London sent Captain James Cook to the Pacific aboard the *Endeavour*, to record the transit of Venus. After completing this task he then voyaged to land that he refers to in his journal as 'New Holland' (which suggests that he wasn't the first European to arrive there), where 'in the greatest plenty is the Kangooroo, or Kanguru so call'd by the Natives; we saw a good many of them about Endeavour River, but kill'd only Three, which we found very good eating.'

In fact, Dutch explorer Willem Janszoon first sighted the coast in 1606 – more than a hundred and fifty years before Cook arrived. In *The Discoverers*, historian Daniel J. Boorstin describes how 'in 1642, Abel Tasman . . . was commissioned by Anton van Diemen, governor-general of the Dutch East Indies, to go exploring to the "Great South Land".' Tasman named one area 'Van Diemen's Land' after his patron; in 1856, it was renamed Tasmania after Tasman himself. So it seems that there were several Europeans to have made it to various parts of Australia before Cook landed on its shores.

Cook wasn't even the first Englishman to reach Australia. Australian studies professor and author of *The Explorers*, Tim F. Flannery, makes the point that it was English adventurer William Dampier who 'provided the first extended account in English of the Great South Land and its inhabitants when he landed on the north-western Australian coast in January 1688', which was about eighty years before Cook's eventual arrival.

Bloomers were invented by Amelia Bloomer

When my niece Isobelle was younger, she used to love the story of how Mrs Bloomer invented bloomers – except when Isobelle told it, Mrs Bloomer used to get called 'Mrs Knickers'. However, neither Mrs Bloomer nor Mrs Knickers invented bloomers. It was Elizabeth Smith Miller.

According to Dale M. Bauer, author of *The Cambridge Companion to Nineteenth-Century American Women's Writing* and a professor of Women's Studies, while frequenting European spas in 1849 American traveller Elizabeth Smith Miller had donned 'a shortened skirt worn over large, so-called "Turkish trowsers", gathered in at the ankle with a string or button'. When Smith Miller got home to the US she made herself a pair. It seems she didn't exactly invent them – just had the nerve to bring the fashion back to the States and go out in them.

Smith Miller describes her motivation thus: 'In the spring of 1851, while spending many hours at work in the garden, I became so thoroughly disgusted with the long skirt that the dissatisfaction, the growth of years, suddenly ripened into the decision that this shackle should no longer be endured.' Her solution to the problem was to wear 'Turkish trousers to the ankle, with a skirt reaching some four inches below the knee'.

Amelia Bloomer, who was an acquaintance of one of Smith Miller's friends, Mrs Stanton, wrote a letter to the Chicago-based *Religio-Philosophical Journal* in 1889, in which she described how 'Elizabeth Smith Miller . . . appeared on the streets of our village dressed in short skirt and full Turkish trousers.'

According to Smith Miller, the reason that the clothing was credited with such a name was because: 'Mrs Bloomer . . . then adopted the dress, and as she was editing a paper in which she advocated it, the dress was christened with her name'. Author of *No Small Courage* Nancy F. Cott confirms that 'the new garment became known as bloomers after editor and temperance advocate Amelia Bloomer described them [in 1851] in the *Lily*, a magazine for women'.

However, Bloomer was adamant that she had never set out to claim the garment as her 'personal invention', and that the popular press was at fault:

At the outset I had no idea of fully adopting the style – no thought of setting a fashion – no thought that my action would create an excitement throughout the civilized world and give to the style my name and the credit due Mrs Miller. This was all the work of the press.

Newfoundland was first discovered by English explorer, John Cabot

Though the name of the fifteenth-century explorer John Cabot sounds English, the *Encyclopaedia Britannica* reliably informs us that 'Giovanni Caboto' was an Italian explorer who moved to Bristol in 1495, where his name became anglicized.

In 1497, while looking for Asia, Cabot happened upon Newfoundland, but he wasn't the first European to reach the area, as Portuguese nobleman João Vaz Corte Real is thought to have discovered Newfoundland in 1472.

If he did, however, he was still way behind previous European discoverers. In *The Oxford History of the Vikings*, professor of medieval history Peter Sawyer describes how 'remains found at L'Anse aux Meadows on the northern tip of Newfoundland are good evidence that Scandinavians who had settled in Greenland reached North America early in the eleventh century'.

Authors of *Atlantic Canada*, Mark Morris and Andrew Hempstead, confirm that 'L'Anse aux Meadows was once a full-fledged Norse village serving as a sailing base for explorations throughout the area about AD 1000,' and they further reveal that 'digs uncovered eight complexes of rudimentary houses, workshops with fireplaces and a trove of artefacts, which verified the Norse presence.'

So it would seem that Signor Caboto was almost five hundred years too late.

The modern flush toilet was invented by Thomas Crapper

According to writer and broadcaster Adam Hart-Davis, author of *Thunder, Flush and Thomas Crapper*: 'During the 1880s various types of siphonic systems were being patented at the rate of about twenty per year – but none by Thomas Crapper.' Rudimentary toilets had already been invented in the 1770s by Alexander Cumming and Joseph Bramah, but it was a Mr Joseph Adamson who took out the first patent for a siphonic flush in 1853.

Thomas Crapper originally hailed from Thorne, near Doncaster, but moved south to London where he became apprenticed to a plumber in Chelsea. From humble beginnings he built up his own plumbing business – Thos

... but how does it fit under the bed?

Crapper & Co. – and as Hart-Davis explains, he was later 'employed by the royal family when they refurbished Sandringham House in the 1880s'. Despite his success in the plumbing world, Crapper was not responsible for inventing the modern flush toilet.

In *W. C. Privy's Original Bathroom Companion*, author Jack Mingo states: 'In 1596, Queen Elizabeth I allowed her godson, Sir John Harrington, to install a flush toilet of his own invention in her living quarters,' but she lived to regret it 'when he published a small promotional booklet about it, making the Queen's toilet the butt of many popular jokes'.

Marry, my good liege, hast thou heard the one about the Queen's toilet . . . ?

Newton discovered the law of gravity when an apple fell on his head

No eighteenth-century writers mention the apple hitting Isaac Newton on the head. In *Isaac Newton*, scientist Michael White quotes contemporary biographer William Stukeley recording in 1726 how the notion of gravitation in Newton's mind was 'occasioned by the fall of an apple as he sat in a contemplative mood'. While a remark from contemporary scientist Henry Pemberton – 'As he [Newton] sat alone in the garden, he fell into a speculation on the power of gravity' – mentions neither an apple nor indeed any other fruit in association with Newton's epiphany.

Biographer and author of *Never At Rest*, Richard S. Westfall, quotes Newton's niece, Mrs Conduitt, who described how, when Newton was musing in a garden, *it came into his thought that the power of gravity (which brought an apple from the tree to the ground) was not limited to a certain distance from the earth, but that this power must extend much farther than was usually thought.*

Westfall claims that the story 'vulgarizes universal gravitation by treating it as a bright idea', and pointing out that 'the stories about the apple and the law of gravity all came from his old age'.

White goes further and suggests that the apple story is 'almost certainly a fabrication . . . designed . . . to suppress the fact that much of the inspiration for the theory of gravity came from his [Newton's] subsequent alchemical work'.

It would appear that a notion as groundbreaking as the theory of gravity probably didn't come to Newton with such ease, and that the apple story was, perhaps, told as an anecdote in his final years.

Nylon is so named because it was invented in New York and London

Textile research tutor Susanna Handley points out in *Nylon* that 'New York (NY) and London (LON) [are] incorrectly believed to be the twin sites of nylon's simultaneous discovery.'

According to the *Encyclopaedia Britannica*, in the 1930s the American company DuPont 'announced the invention of the first wholly synthetic fibre . . . polyhexamethylene adipamide'. But women could hardly be expected to go up to the counter and request a pair of polyhexamethylene adipamides so, as the 1978 DuPont publication

Context explains, the name 'No-Run' was chosen. It was thought to be misleading, however, so the DuPont management team changed one letter at a time until the word 'Nylon' was finally approved.

Handley provides a little more detail, and explains that 'in the light of tests showing that Fiber 66 did run', the brand name 'No-Run' was rendered slightly inaccurate, so they spelt it backwards: 'Nuron'. This sounded too much like a nerve tonic so the 'r' was changed to an 'l' to make 'Nulon'. 'New Nulon' sounded awkward so the 'u' was changed to an 'i' to make 'Nilon'. However, it was felt that the product might be mispronounced as 'Nillon' so the 'i' was changed to a 'y' to give 'Nylon'. At last! There must have been some aching heads in the DuPont office that morning.

Interestingly, Handley also points out that the word 'nylon' became the generic term for polyamide fibre but 'it was never patented as a trademark by DuPont.'

The steam engine was invented by James Watt

James Scott's engraving *Watt's First Experiment With Steam* shows James Watt (1736–1819) as a child, observing a steaming kettle. Mrs Campbell, James Watt's cousin and companion, recounted in her memoranda of 1798:

Sitting one evening with his aunt, Mrs Muirhead, at the tea table, she said: 'James Watt, I never saw such an idle boy; take a book or employ yourself usefully; for the last hour you have not spoken one word, but taken off the lid of that kettle and put it on again, holding now a cup and now a silver spoon over the steam, watching how it rises from the spout, and catching and connecting the drops of hot water it falls into. Are you not ashamed of spending your time in this way?'

Though it cannot be proven whether the young James Watt really was obsessed by the kettle boiling on the hearth, there is no doubt that he played a key role in the development of steam power in later life. However, credit for creating the first successful steam engine must go to Thomas Newcomen, who built his first machine in Staffordshire in 1712, twenty-four years before Watt was even born.

According to author Richard L. Hills in *Power From Steam*, Newcomen's engine 'remained virtually unaltered until the vital inventions of James Watt'. He further makes the point that 'no one could have imagined that, when Professor James Anderson asked Watt to repair a model of an atmospheric engine . . . it would be a turning point in the history of civilization.'

In 1763, Watt began improvements to Newcomen's design by fitting a separate condenser through which steam from the cylinder was passed and cooled, allowing the engine to remain hot, and so reducing fuel consumption. In 1769, Watt patented his separate condensing chamber for the steam engine and the Industrial Revolution was born.

The telephone was invented by Alexander Graham Bell

In *Everything's Relative*, physicist Tony Rothman points out that in 1861, German physicist Johann Philipp Reis 'attempted electrical voice transmission well over a decade before Bell' and produced a device called the 'Telephon'. Author John Bankston backs up this view in *Alexander Graham Bell and the Story of the Telephone*, describing Reis's 'Telephon' as a device 'that can transmit electrical tones through wires'.

In 2003, John Liffen, Curator of Communications at the Science Museum in London, discovered documents which revealed that an 1863 version of Philipp Reis's telephone was tested by Standard Telephones and Cables (STC) in 1947 and found to be able to transmit and reproduce speech of good quality but of low efficiency. Liffen states that: 'If by telephone, an electrical device is meant that could communicate over a distance greater than that of human hearing, then Reis did invent the telephone.'

According to the author of *Voice Over DSL*, Richard Grigonis, it is supposed that the first words sent by Reis were 'A horse does not eat a cucumber salad,' which is certainly more cryptic than Alexander Graham Bell's, 'Mr Watson – come here – I want you.'

Grigonis also reveals that twelve years before Johann Philipp Reis invented the Telephon, Italian inventor Antonio Meucci designed what he called the 'speaking telegraph', which he built in Havana in 1849. John Bankston supports this view, and has written that 'Many people believe that that honour [of inventing the telephone] belongs to Antonio Meucci.' Indeed, United States Congress Resolution 269 (11 June 2002) states:

Expressing the sense of the House of Representatives to honour the life and achievements of Nineteenth-Century Italian-American inventor Antonio Meucci, and his work in the invention of the telephone . . . [he worked] with

ceaseless vigour on . . . an invention he later called the
'teletrofono', involving electronic communications.

Neither Reis's nor Meucci's prototypes caught on, and were largely forgotten. Liffen rightly points out that 'the process of invention does not stop at a successful demonstration, and it was Bell and his associates who made the telephone a practical and commercial success,' and, as a result, became very, very rich.

Thomas Edison invented the electric light

The development of electric light may well have ended with Thomas Edison, but it began with Sir Humphry Davy, and owes a great deal to many unsung heroes in between.

Edison's biographer Frank Lewis Dyer suggests that 'all may be referred back to the brilliant demonstrations of Sir Humphry Davy at the Royal Institution, *circa* 1809–10.' Writing in *Edison*, Dyer describes how 'with the current from a battery of two thousand cells he [Davy] produced an intense voltaic arc between the points of consuming sticks of charcoal.'

Author of *They All Laughed: From Light Bulbs to Lasers,* Ira Flatow claims that 'at least three or four serious inventors, in England, France, and the United States, were working on the incandescent lamp in the 1870s.' These included Heinrich Göbel, who built a functioning light bulb thirty years earlier, and Joseph Swan who, as Flatow points out, 'designed an incandescent lamp using carbon shaped into the form of a cylinder.'

According to Flatow, Edison admitted to having read an article by Joseph Swan, which detailed his discoveries, with the result that 'Swan defenders claim Edison stole this idea from Swan [and] Edison backers claim Edison read the article after he designed his own carbon filament.'

By 1879 what Edison ended up with was the commercially viable 'Edison modern incandescent lamp' – or the light bulb, to you and me.

Magellan circumnavigated the world

Sixteenth-century Portuguese navigator and explorer Ferdinand Magellan circumnavigated the world in spirit, perhaps, but not in body.

On 10 August 1519, Magellan set out from Seville with 260 men and a fleet of five ships: the *Trinidad* (Magellan's flagship), the *San Antonio*, the *Concepción*, the *Victoria* and the *Santiago*. By the time he had entered the Pacific Ocean (which he so named because it appeared so still and peaceful), he had only three of these ships left. In April 1521, a year and eight months after setting sail, Magellan landed in the Philippines and was killed in a fight with natives on Mactan Island, a year and five months before the circumnavigation would eventually be completed.

Navigator Antonio Pigafetta recorded in his journal on 27 April 1521:

> One of them [the natives] wounded him on the left leg with a large cutlass, which resembles a scimitar, only being larger. That caused the captain to fall face downward, when immediately they rushed upon him with iron and bamboo spears and with their cutlasses, until they killed our mirror, our light, our comfort, and our true guide.

Pigafetta returned to Spain on 6 September 1522. He was one of only eighteen of Magellan's crew who managed to do so on the one remaining ship, *Victoria*, thanks to the skills of 'the Basque navigator Juan Sebastián de Elcano (del Cano)', which makes de Elcano the first person to circumnavigate the world.

Dr Guillotin invented the guillotine

Contrary to what one might think, Dr Joseph-Ignace Guillotin was a kindly humanitarian. He didn't invent the guillotine, but merely gave it his name.

In *The Days of the French Revolution*, Christopher Hibbert points out that in the sixteenth century such contraptions were already in existence in Germany and Italy, 'as well as in Yorkshire in England where it was known as the Halifax gibbet, and in Scotland where it was called the Maiden'.

The *Encyclopaedia Britannica* explains that, at first, the French version 'was called *Louisette*, or *Louison*' after Antoine Louis, the French surgeon who designed it. Two fourteen-foot uprights were joined by a crossbar at the top and mounted on a platform. The inside edges of the device were greased with tallow. The straight or curved blade was weighted and operated by a rope and pulley system. Later, an angled blade was fitted to replace the straight or curved one.

In 1789, Guillotin, a Deputy of Paris in the Assemblée Constituante, suggested using the Louisette on humanitarian grounds, so that, according to *Britannica*, 'the privilege of execution by decapitation would no longer be confined to the nobles.' Guillotin was opposed to the death penalty and hoped that a more humane method of execution would be the first step towards abolition of the practice.

Unfortunately, his descendants weren't too happy that the device became referred to as the 'guillotine' and they promptly changed their surname.

15

Language and Grammar

'Aluminum' is an American corruption of 'aluminium'

In 1808, when English chemist Sir Humphry Davy first isolated this element, he chose to call it 'alumium', because of its association with the sulphate 'alum', but as *The Good Word Guide* reveals, four years later he had a change of heart, and gave it the name 'aluminum'.

Though 'aluminum' was a name readily adopted in the United States, the use of the word in Britain was largely opposed in scientific and establishment circles. In the *Bloomsbury Dictionary of Word Origins* lexicographer John Ayto cites the *Quarterly Review* of 1812 as clearly preferring the alternative 'Aluminium, for so we shall take the liberty of writing the word, in preference to aluminum, which has a less classical sound.'

In other words, the British Establishment altered the chosen name in favour of one that matched up with the endings of names of other established elements, such as magnesium, potassium and sodium.

'Beg the question' means 'raise the question'

To 'beg the question' is a catchy phrase beloved by journalists and interviewers, but did you know that it has a specific meaning all to itself and is often misused? Strictly speaking, it is not interchangeable with to 'raise the question' or to 'prompt the question'.

According to pedantic grammarians, 'beg' in this sense has a different meaning from 'humbly request'. *Fowler's Modern Usage* explains that in strict usage it is 'the English equivalent of the Latin *petitio principii*', which, according to *The Good Word Guide*, means 'to base an argument on an assumption whose truth is the very thing that is being disputed'. For example, the statement, 'It's true that I did not steal the money since I cannot possibly be lying' is 'begging' the question. i.e., if my honesty is the very topic in dispute, I can hardly call upon it to prove my case.

If you want to point out that a statement raises questions, a phrase such as 'that raises the question as to where all the money has gone' is correct, rather than 'that begs the question as to where all the money has gone'.

'Gotten' is an American corruption of 'got'

The word 'gotten' is in fact Middle English and comes from the Old Norse *geta*.

Its use was employed by William Shakespeare in *Henry VI, Part Three*, which was first printed in 1623, when

Warwick says: 'You told not how Henry the Sixth hath lost all that which Henry the Fifth had gotten?'

The Concise Oxford Dictionary of Word Origins tells us that the clipped form 'got' dates from 1600, though eighteenth-century Anglo-Irish author Jonathan Swift and nineteenth-century Scottish author Sir Walter Scott both tended to use 'gotten'.

Though it might appear that 'begotten', 'forgotten' and 'ill-gotten' are relics from this time, they are compound words from the Germanic *gietan*. They pre-date the Middle English 'gotten' and are classed as Old English.

Did you know ... ?

The Good Word Guide explains that '"it's" [is] a contraction of "it is"' whereas '"its" is the possessive form of "it"' and therefore that 'the insertion of an apostrophe in the possessive for "its" is wrong in all contexts.'

For example, 'It's aim is to encourage better English' literally means 'It is aim is to encourage better English,' which is incorrect, and should properly read, 'Its aim is to encourage better English.'

The first line of the carol reads 'God rest ye, merry gentlemen'

Dodgy punctuation is the culprit behind this fallacy. The sentiment being conveyed isn't one of hope that God will allow these cheery chaps a bit of a kip; instead we are trusting he will 'rest them merry': that is '*keep* them merry'. The comma should come *after* merry rather than before.

From the fifteenth century, 'rest' had two different meanings: 'repose' from Old German and 'remain' from the Old French *rester*, as in the phrase 'rest assured' and 'rest easy'.

When punctuated correctly, therefore, the line reads: 'God rest ye merry, gentlemen.'

Never end a sentence with a preposition

This grammar 'rule' dates back to seventeenth-century English poet and essayist John Dryden. In *Grammar for Smart People*, Barry Tarshis explains that 'Dryden based his view on the fact that prepositions are never found at the end of sentences written in Latin.'

Tarshis also makes the point that:

Neither Dryden nor the grammarians who promoted his views envisioned the extent to which many of the most commonly used prepositions – on, to, in, about, over, of, etc. – would hook up with verbs to become common idioms . . . Nor did they take into account the awkwardness that results when you run one of these verb-preposition idioms through the never-end-a-sentence-with-a-preposition wringer.

The eighteenth-century bishop Robert Lowth upheld the 'rule' by urging readers not to end sentences with a preposition if they could decently avoid it. In modern times, however, *The Good Word Guide* states that although a Latin sentence cannot end with a preposition, there is no reason why this should have any implication for English usage.

According to *The Oxford Companion to the English Language*, when Winston Churchill read in a government report a clumsy attempt to rearrange a sentence so that it wouldn't end with a preposition, he famously scribbled in the margin: 'This is the sort of bloody nonsense up with which I will not put.'

Fowler's describes the not-ending-a-sentence-with-a-preposition myth as 'one of the most persistent myths about prepositions in English'. I wonder what all the others are.

'Fall' is American English for 'autumn'

In fourteenth-century English, the third season of the year was called 'autumn' from the Latin *autumnus*. By the sixteenth century, the terms 'fall of the leaf' or 'fall' had become standard in England and likewise in America from the late seventeenth century.

However, in Britain, around 1800, 'autumn' regained popularity and has remained as standard ever since, while the Americans continue to use the English sixteenth-century word 'fall'.

'Decimate' means 'annihilate'

According to *The Good Word Guide* the word decimate has become associated with annihilation and mass destruction because of the 'mistaken belief that the word means to destroy all but a tenth'.

In fact, decimate means to 'destroy one in ten, from the Roman practice of killing every tenth soldier as a punishment for mutiny'.

16

Mammals

Bats are blind

The reason that bats use echolocation to get around is not because they can't see, but because they are nocturnal but can't see in the dark. In *Owls Aren't Wise and Bats Aren't Blind*, naturalist Warner Shedd reveals that 'no bats are blind, and most actually see quite well.' Because even the best night vision has serious limitations, Shedd points out that, instead, 'bats rely on a most remarkable system, similar to radar or sonar, known as echolocation.'

Author of *Bats of the World* Dr Gary L. Graham refutes the belief that bats are blind: 'All bats can see, and many have excellent vision.' Indeed, the *Encyclopaedia Britannica* makes the point that: 'The Old World bats [*Megachiroptera*] . . . rely on vision rather than echolocation (animal sonar) as a means of avoiding obstacles.'

Milk is good for cats

Veterinary surgeon Aileen Brown from the Caledonian Cat Clinic in Edinburgh explains that 'some [cats] have an inability to digest lactose, a sugar which is found in cows' milk,' which will result in the poor animal suffering from diarrhoea. However, there are some cat-milk products

that are available which have had the lactose removed. Brown suggests that milk is best regarded as 'an occasional treat for your cat rather than a regular food supplement'.

In *Guide To a Healthy Cat*, Dr Elaine Wexler-Mitchell warns cat owners that although felines 'love the taste of cow's milk, cats are fairly lactose intolerant'. Wexler-Mitchell agrees with Aileen Brown that because cats 'lack the enzyme needed to properly digest the sugar found in cow's milk . . . more than a taste or two will usually cause diarrhoea'.

Echoing the views of Brown and Wexler-Mitchell, vet Dan Rice goes further in *The Complete Book of Cat Breeding,* and claims that 'milk should never be included in a feline diet. It is dangerous, even when fed in small quantities.'

The next time your cat brushes up against you in the hope of receiving a creamy dish of cow's milk, it might be better to harden your heart and ignore its plaintive mews . . . (Incidentally, the same holds true for ailing hedgehogs, who benefit more from a nice tin of dog food than from a diarrhoea-inducing plate of bread and milk.)

Lemmings commit mass suicide

Contrary to popular belief, lemmings do not, en masse, lose the will to live and plunge into the sea in a deliberate suicidal fashion. Rather, the *Encyclopaedia Britannica* explains, if a colony becomes overcrowded 'lemmings may migrate' and some may 'drown when they are pushed into the sea by the pressing momentum of the masses behind them'.

In *Mammals of North America* wildlife experts Roland W. Kays and Don E. Wilson describe how 'in good years, their populations can explode and large numbers of animals can be seen running across the low tundra, dispersing out of overpopulated areas.' It is this unusual sight that they believe 'has led to the myth of suicidal, cliff-jumping lemmings'.

The belief appears to have been prevalent in Victorian times since Llewellyn Lloyd, writing in *Scandinavian Adventures (Volume 2)* published in 1854, details the event then questions its voracity, stating 'it is not credible to me that when an army of lemmings thus launches forth on the wide ocean; it is with the intention of committing suicide.' In the twentieth century, the erroneous belief was reinforced with Disney's 1958 *White Wilderness* film, which was part of the studio's 'True Life Adventure' series, in which narrator Winston Hibler described how: 'A kind of compulsion seizes each tiny rodent and, carried along by an unreasoning hysteria, each falls into step for a march that will take them to a strange destiny.' Strange indeed, considering that no wildlife expert has *ever* discovered conclusive evidence that proves that lemmings are prone to such bizarre behaviour.

Much misunderstood, it would seem that these furry hamster-like creatures are *not* the most depressed mammals on the planet, which is good to know.

Adult male gorillas have hairy chests

Human hairy chests are often likened to those of gorillas. Indeed, 'gorilla' even means 'hairy person'. Nature, on the other hand, seems to be working in the opposite fashion in men and gorillas, as Dr J. Bryan Carroll, Deputy Director of Bristol Zoo, points out that 'young gorillas . . . do have hairs on their chests [whereas] . . . adult male gorillas have a hairless chest.'

In *Gorillas*, author Seymour Simon explains that 'an adult gorilla has hair all over its body except for its face, its chest, and the palms of its hands and soles of its feet.'

Next time you are tempted to compare a human hairy chest to that of a gorilla, bear in mind that gorillas' chests are noted for being remarkably bald.

Did you know . . . ?

Whale expert and author of *The Whale Family Book*, Cynthia D'Vincent explains that contrary to popular belief, whales do not blow water from their blow holes. 'Early whalers believed the blow was a spout of water, but actually it is a cloud of moist used-up air that a whale pushes out of its lungs.'

In *The Blue Whale*, author Christine Corning Malloy reveals that whales breathe through two blowholes or nostrils which are found on the tops of their heads: 'When the moisture in the warm exhaled air hits the cold ocean air it creates water vapour that rises in a spectacular slender column called a "blow".'

One dog year equals seven human years

Twenty-seven-year-old Border collie Bramble, from Bridg-water, Somerset is one of the world's oldest dogs. By the above method of reckoning, she's reached the grand old age of 189, but dog breeder and author of *Guide to Owning an Ageing Dog* Yvonne Kejcz states that in modern times 'this equation is no longer believed to be valid.'

Writing in *The Dog Owner's Manual*, vet David Brunner highlights the popular misconception that dogs age seven years for each calendar year, and makes the point that 'canine ageing is much more rapid during the first two years of a dog's life'. In reality, the rate of ageing in dogs differs according to breed and size. Brunner explains:

> *After the first two years the ratio settles down to five to one for small and medium breeds. For large breeds the rate is six to one, and for giant breeds the rate is seven to one. Thus, at ten years of age a Great Dane would be eighty years old, while a pug would only be sixty-four.*

In their book *The Good Life: Your Dog's First Year*, Mordecai Siegal and Matthew Margolis point out that the seven to one dog-year formula cannot compute properly for a number of reasons; particularly because 'it does not take into consideration that the first year of a dog's life is the equivalent to the first eighteen years of a child's life.'

Author of *Puppy Care and Training* Bardi McLennan reveals that there are several variations of more accurate formulas. For example: 'One dog year equals fifteen human; two dog years equals twenty-four human. Then add four years to the human's for every one of the dog's.'

Though the new formula is a little more tricky to remember, at least it knocks years off Bramble, making her a spritely 124 years old, rather than an aged 189!

Giant pandas are from the racoon family and are vegetarian

Though it's hard to believe, for more than a century, scientists were undecided as to whether the giant panda and red panda were members of the bear family or the racoon family. According to the authors of *Of Pandas and People*, Percival Davis and Dean H. Kenyon: 'About half the studies done on the pandas concluded that they are bears; half concluded that they are racoons.' Davis and Kenyon reveal that a study conducted in 1964 eventually came to the conclusion that is now generally accepted as the definitive interpretation: 'The giant panda is a bear.'

Further confirmation was given during the 1990s following the publication of improved molecular analyses, which, according to the *Encyclopaedia Britannica*, 'strongly suggest bears as the giant panda's closest relatives'. The red panda, it appears, is neither bear nor racoon and has been reclassified into a family of its own.

As for the eating habits of pandas, everyone had believed that giant pandas were exclusively vegetarian until farmers in China started missing the odd goat. It later transpired that local pandas were eating them. *Britannica* explains that 'pandas retain a taste for meat, which is used as bait to capture them for radio collaring and has made them pests in human camps on occasion.'

Giant-panda expert George B. Schaller, author of *Giant Pandas*, also confirms that pandas are not exclusively vegetarians: 'Although bamboo comprises more than ninety-nine per cent of its diet, the panda's taste for meat is quite well documented.'

Pigs are sweaty animals, hence the saying 'to sweat like a pig'

Anthropologist and author of the unusually titled *Cows, Pigs, Wars, and Witches: The Riddles of Culture*, Marvin Harris knowledgeably informs us that 'pigs can't sweat'. In fact, according to Harris, the sweatiest of all mammals are human beings!

If a pig is exposed to direct sunlight and air temperatures of more than 98°F, it has to 'dampen its skin with external moisture', and generally prefers to do this by 'wallowing in fresh clean mud'.

Pet-pig expert Priscilla Valentine explains in *Potbellied Pig Behaviour and Training* that 'the pig has virtually no sweat glands to keep him cool. The mud acts as a natural skin conditioner . . . and as a bug repellent and sunscreen.'

The late Victorians were the first to exclaim 'I'm sweating like a pig!' An equally popular expression of the day was 'I'm sweating like a bull', according to *Cassell's Dictionary of Slang*. The Victorians were half right as cattle do sweat, but pigs, which originate from shadier climes, do not. Unfortunately for the reputation of the blameless pig, it is the former expression that has endured.

17
Grooming

Hair can turn white overnight

In his book *Biological Perspectives on Human Pigmentation*, clinical pharmacologist Ashley H. Robins cites some famous historical examples, including Sir Thomas More, whose hair and beard appeared to turn white on the night before his execution. Similarly, Marie Antoinette's hair is reputed to have turned white after she was 'reviled and abused by the ferocious mob in the most unfeeling manner' during the French Revolution, as described by the 1850 *National Cyclopaedia of Useful Knowledge*.

However, in Dr John Gray's *The World of Hair*, it is explained that 'a black hair cannot of itself suddenly turn white . . . Hairs grow for years with pigment inside them, and since they are "dead" there is no process by which the melanin throughout a hair can be naturally destroyed rapidly.' So how can a full head of hair appear to turn white overnight without a single hair changing its colour?

Marilyn Sherlock, chairman of the Institute of Trichologists, reveals that the illusion of hair turning completely white is due to a disorder called *alopecia areata*: 'Sometimes this condition attacks only pigmented hairs. If the person is grey (a combination of their natural colour and white) the dark hairs can literally fall out overnight. This leaves only the white hairs remaining.'

Science writer Christopher Wanjek also agrees that the condition, which can be stress-related, can cause pigmented hair to fall out, over a two-week period, so that only white hairs are left behind.

As for the reasons behind Sir Thomas More's overnight hair whitening, imminent decapitation would be stressful enough to prompt anybody's hair to fall out!

Eating jelly cubes aids nail growth

Eating a cube of jelly a day is a longstanding home remedy for strengthening nails. The reasoning behind this is because one of the ingredients in jelly is gelatine, which, according to the *Encyclopaedia Britannica*, is a protein derived from collagen that is 'found in animal skin and bone [and] is extracted by boiling animal hides, skins, bones and tissue'.

The belief that gelatine can strengthen nails dates back to the 1950s. In her book *Eve-olution*, business writer Faith Popcorn reveals that a dietary supplement in the form of a gelatine preparation, 'Knox for Nails', was launched at this time, followed by Cutex's 'Nail Strengthener with Knox Gelatine', which was applied directly to the nails.

Professor of Dermatology at Columbia University, Richard K. Scher, states that 'it has never been proven in a controlled and scientific fashion that gelatine does anything to strengthen nails.'

Anti-ageing creams work

Consumers' Association magazine *Which?* conducted a double-blind survey in 1998 in which ninety-six women tested ordinary moisturizers against anti-ageing creams. Announcing its results, *Which?* stated: 'Our four-week trial revealed that women couldn't tell whether they were using an ordinary moisturizer or an anti-ageing one.'

The findings produced by *Which?* concluded that 'some of the claims made for the ingredients of anti-ageing creams can be substantiated but, in the low concentrations used in the creams, they are unlikely to do more than moisturize your skin.'

According to dermatology professor Christopher Griffiths: 'Despite the huge resources invested in researching the "fountain of youth", most anti-ageing remedies are little better than expensive moisturizers.' Instead he recommends 'effective use of sunscreens of factor fifteen or more' to help maintain one's youthful appearance.

Wet shaving should be performed against the hair growth

Many men shave against the direction of hair growth assuming they will get a smoother result. The experts, however, claim that all this will achieve is a nasty case of 'razor burn'.

US manufacturer of surgical preparation razors, Derma-Safe, place most importance on the direction in which the blade is stroked:

When the stroking is in the direction of the lay of the hair, the hair is readily trapped against the skin and cut ... When stroking is against the lay of the hair, the hair is initially lifted up by the blade and tipped against the skin. This has the effect of raising the skin behind the hair; when the hair is penetrated this mound of skin is sheared off – causing increased damage to the epidermis and dulling the blade.

Geo F. Trumper, a traditional gentlemen's barbers based in London, is in full agreement, advising its male customers to shave in the direction of the beard growth: 'Never shave "against the grain" of the beard as this pulls the skin in the wrong direction causing small cuts and grazing to the skin, and is the most common cause of razor burn.'

The Gentleman's Shop in Hungerford, Berkshire, confirms that a man should always shave 'with the lie of the beard, never against'.

All three expert companies also emphasize the importance of using a good sharp blade.

White marks on the nails indicate lack of calcium

Professor of dermatology Nelson Lee Novick reveals that in the developing world, among people who are poorly nourished, 'certain nutritional deficiencies, particularly a lack of zinc or protein in your diet, can cause a nearly total whiteout of your nail except for the tips, or even a pattern of white bands across the width of the nail'. In the Western world, however, Novick points out that most white marks on nails are due to 'mild trauma – such as hitting or slamming your fingernail on or into something'.

The New York Nail Company states that the white marks that appear on finger nails are not the sign of calcium deficiency: 'White marks appear when a trauma has occurred to the nail plate . . . A knock to the nail plate can create air pockets in the surface, which appear as white marks.'

In *Standard Nail Technology*, cosmetologist Sue Ellen Schultes confirms this by explaining that the white marks, known as 'leukonychia', are generally caused by 'air bubbles, a bruise, or other injury to the nail'.

So if you do spot the odd little white mark appearing on a finger nail, it's not a sign that you have to drink a pint of milk a day or that you need to start consuming calcium supplements: chances are you've injured your finger without realizing it!

18

Medical Matters

Anorexia is a slimmers' disease

Though anorexia is known colloquially as the 'slimmers' disease', this title is misleading, and does not give a useful or accurate description of the condition, which is very serious, and not merely an obsession with weight or slimming. As the *Family Encyclopedia of Medicine and Health* points out, the cause of anorexia is 'far more complex that the simple desire to lose weight'.

According to Anorexia Bulimia Care UK, the medical label, 'anorexia nervosa' is also less than helpful for those trying to understand the condition:

The term literally means 'loss of appetite from nervous origins', but the patient has usually conquered her appetite, not lost it . . . Although she may claim at the time to have no appetite, many recovered patients admit that they were often extremely hungry but refused themselves the right to eat.

NHS Direct states that although the disease has partial connections with 'the modern importance on being thin', 'the causes of anorexia nervosa . . . are also linked to feelings of control and self-worth'. A factsheet issued by

BUPA backs up this view, and suggests that 'weight control may be used as a substitute for gaining control in other areas of life.'

An eyeball can be removed, washed and replaced by a medical expert

One sometimes hears astonishing stories about a paramedic or first-aider who has saved someone's eyesight by whipping out the eyeball, rinsing it free from a foreign body and popping it back in. Amazing though it sounds, it is completely impossible.

Consultant ophthalmologist R. D. Daniel of Moorfield's Eye Hospital in London explains why:

The eye is attached to the brain by the optic nerve. The optic nerve is comprised of bundles of nerve fibres surrounding very important blood vessels and cannot be stretched . . . There is certainly not enough slack to allow an eye to be removed from the socket without causing permanent harm to the nerve.

Daniel clarifies the matter once and for all with the assertion that 'the only time an eye would be removed from the socket would be to remove it permanently.'

Animal fur and dust cause allergies

Many people who suffer with nasal or breathing allergies assume that their pets' fur is the cause of their symptoms. However, according to Ellen Mazo, co-author of *The Immune Advantage*, the real culprit is 'a protein released with the animals' dander (dead skin cells) and saliva'. In smaller pets, the allergen can be in urine and so their bedding can develop into a reservoir for the allergen.

In *Rex Cats: A Complete Pet Owner's Manual*, cat specialist J. Anne Helgren also confirms that it isn't animal fur that causes the problem where allergies are concerned. Rather, it's an allergenic protein called 'Fel d1' which is found in cat saliva, and which is deposited on skin and fur when a cat cleans itself: 'When cats groom, they spread this protein on to their fur, whether it's straight, curly, wavy, or absent altogether.'

On a point of interest, Dr Laurence A. Smolley reveals in *Breathe Right Now* that 'female cats produced one-third fewer allergy-causing proteins . . . than the males.'

Likewise, it's not dust or even dust mites to which most asthma sufferers are sensitive. Author of *Hay Fever* Dr Jonathan Brostoff explains that it's 'a digestive enzyme . . . found on the mite's droppings'. In his book *The Allergy and Asthma Cure*, Dr Fred Pescatore confirms that the droppings of dust mites (which live in house dust) are 'the most common triggers of perennial allergy and asthma symptoms such as a congested or runny nose; itchy, watery eyes; coughing; and wheezing'.

Schizophrenia is a condition involving split personality

The Greek prefix *schiz* means 'split' as in 'schism', but as Rethink (the body formerly known as the National Schizophrenia Fellowship) explains, the 'split' stands for the way that 'thought, feeling and intention' are fragmented. It does not imply a sectioning up of personality into different aspects such as a timid personality and an aggressive personality.

A state in which distinct personalities form is a very rare (and, in some quarters, disputed) condition currently known as Dissociative Identity Disorder. It has, as Rethink points out, 'nothing to do with schizophrenia'.

Flat-footed candidates are prevented from joining the army

According to orthopaedic surgeon M. David Tremaine, co-author of *The Foot and Ankle Sourcebook*: 'People with flat feet have minimal or no arch in the foot and the arch lies flat against the floor.' Flat feet are also known as 'fallen arches' or *Pes planus*.

In *Pain Free*, author Pete Egoscue explains that without the arch the foot 'has no shock-absorbing capacity ... which means that as the dysfunctional foot strikes the ground, it sends the impact waves right up the bones of the lower leg to the knee and beyond'. This can lead to foot-ache and pains in the leg, and can make it difficult to march properly.

However, according to the British Army website, if, during examination, candidates are found to have flat feet and the doctor believes them 'capable of undergoing training', candidates may still be 'eligible to join'.

If a shingles rash meets in the middle, the patient dies

Shingles is caused by the varicella-zoster virus, and is a rash that spreads around the lower abdomen. In *Varicella-Zoster Virus* it is revealed that the word shingles 'derives from the Medieval Latin word *cingulus*, a girdle', which refers to the shape of the rash, which follows the patterns of nerve supply to the skin.

The Family Encyclopedia of Medicine and Health states that, with regard to the illness, 'there is no truth in the belief that, if a band of rash meets in the middle, the patient will die'.

Dr John Murtagh, Professor of General Practice at Monash University in Australia is in full agreement. He describes the myth as 'nonsense'.

Back pain responds to bed rest

The National Back Pain Association, BackCare, states that for sufferers of back pain, 'bed rest is not recommended and makes matters worse and so should be avoided.' According to recent research, patients who return to normal activities instead of taking to their bed for long periods 'feel healthier, take fewer painkillers, and are less distressed than those who limit their activities'.

The British Chiropractic Association is in full support of this view, and promotes the idea that people should stay active during their recovery from back pain, as 'prolonged bed rest weakens the bones and muscles and reduces your chances of a full recovery'.

A Finnish research team, led by A. Malmivaara in 1995, found that in the treatment of acute low back pain, recovery was slowest among the patients assigned to bed rest. Their findings, published in the *New England Journal of Medicine*, led them to the conclusion that patients with acute low back pain got better faster by 'continuing ordinary activities within the limits permitted by the pain'.

Ingrown toenails grow into the toe

NHS Direct states that the term 'ingrown' gives the wrong impression, as the growth of the toenail is quite normal, and doesn't grow into the tissues. NHS

Direct explains how the problem arises: 'In this condition there is inflammation of the soft tissues surrounding the nail, following infection . . . this leads to . . . swelling . . . [which] . . . overlaps the edge of the nail causing it to look as if the nail has grown into the tissue.'

Professor Norman L. Browse agrees with the NHS and refers to the term 'ingrowing toenail' as 'a misnomer'. In *An Introduction to the Symptoms and Signs of Surgical Disease,* Browse explains that the sides of the toenail only 'appear' to be 'growing or digging into the substance of the toe'. In reality, 'the nail . . . is growing normally' and it is 'the irregular edge which is damaging the skin'.

How does the edge of the toenail become irregular in the first place? Professor in Child Health and Paediatrics, T. J. David, reveals that the main cause is 'compression of the toe from the side due to ill-fitting footwear'. He adds, too, that 'cutting off the toenails in a half circle instead of straight across' is also to blame.

Colds and pneumonia are caused by being caught in the rain

The days of being able to blame being drenched in an unexpected downpour for causing a bout of sniffles are over. NHS Direct states that it is only viruses that can do this: 'Cold weather itself is not a cause of colds.'

The Common Cold Centre at Cardiff University backs up this view and makes the point that 'There is no scientific evidence that chilling the body causes an increased susceptibility to infection or an increase in the severity of symptoms.'

In *Bad Medicine*, science writer Christopher Wanjek

also states that: 'Cold viruses are the true and only cause of colds . . . If there is no virus around, you won't catch a cold or pneumonia, no matter how soaked you are.' To prove his point, Wanjek explains that 'scientists in Antarctica and in the Arctic rarely have colds because there are few people around to spread a cold virus.'

Dr Robert Bradsher, specialist in infectious diseases at the University of Arkansas for Medical Sciences, reveals that 'viruses, including influenza, are very infectious and are transmitted from one person to the next by touching something that has had the respiratory virus on it and then touching your eye or nose or mouth.' Bradsher adds that one of the best ways to avoid getting a cold is to 'wash your hands or use an alcohol-based hand-washing solution'.

Starve a fever

The Cold and Flu Council states that the 'starve a fever' notion has no basis in medical advice: 'Anyone suffering from a cold or any feverish condition should drink plenty of fluids and eat whatever and whenever they feel the need.'

In fact, according to Dr Kern from the University of Arkansas for Medical Sciences: 'Not only is it a bad idea to starve a fever, it will hinder your ability to recover from the cold.'

In *How to Raise a Healthy Child*, Dr Robert Mendelsohn advises his readers to ignore the old wives' tale 'feed a cold and starve a fever' because in his professional opinion, 'nourishment is an important part of recovery from any illness.' He adds that both colds and fevers burn up calories which need to be replaced, and advises: 'To the extent your child will tolerate it, you should feed both colds and fevers.'

The saying has variations: 'Starve to mean eat plenty if you have a cold to avoid a fever developing. Either way, the above advice still holds good: take nourishment if you can.

19

Sayings

'If you think that, you have another thing coming' means 'You are mistaken'

This oft-heard line may indeed mean 'have a rethink', but people with a fondness for using it ought to be the ones to re-think. *Fowler's Modern English Usage* reveals that the correct form of the second half of the phrase is 'you have another think coming'.

Reasons for the confusion may be twofold: firstly, in speech, the 'k' of think is easily run into the 'c' of coming, and secondly, as *Fowler's* points out, the use of 'think' as a noun is relatively new, being labelled as 'colloquial' as recently as 1993 in the *New Shorter Oxford Dictionary*.

'As fit as a fiddle' means 'in excellent health'

This common saying dates back to the sixteenth century, when Thomas Nashe recorded the expression 'As right as a fiddle'. However, originally the expression had nothing to do with health and everything to do with appropriateness. This is because 'fit', as explained in *Dr Johnson's Dictionary* of 1814, meant 'proper'. We still retain the original meaning in 'fit for a king'. 'Fit' has only meant 'in good shape' since the nineteenth century.

The original meaning of 'as fit as a fiddle', therefore, was 'as appropriate as can be' rather than 'in excellent health'.

The darkest hour is just before the dawn

The seventeenth-century English historian Thomas Fuller said: 'It is always darkest just before the day dawneth' in his descriptive geography of the Holy Land, *A Pisgah – Sight of Palestine*.

However, astronomers David K. Lynch and William Livingston set the record straight in their book, *Colour and Light in Nature*: 'The sun is farthest below the horizon halfway between sunset and sunrise', making the darkest hour the mid-point between these two times. Meteorologist Keith C. Heidorn agrees that the old saying is 'erroneous', and points out that 'the darkest time is at mid-night (not midnight), the halfway point between sunset and sunrise.'

Lynch and Livingston suggest that the belief in 'maximum darkness just before dawn may come from a secondary association of darkness with cold', revealing that 'it truly is coldest just before dawn. But not darkest.'

'Rule of thumb' has its origins in wife-beating

It is regularly claimed that this term comes from an old English law, which cited that a husband was permitted to beat his wife so long as he did it with a stick that was no wider than his thumb. The law is supposedly referred to in Sir William Blackstone's *Commentaries on the Laws of England 1765–1769,* but in *Who Stole Feminism?* philosophy professor Christina Hoff Sommers denies that any reference to such a practice can be found in Blackstone's treatise on English common law: 'On the contrary, British law since the 1700s and . . . American laws predating the Revolution prohibit wife-beating.'

Indeed, the term was in use in the previous century – as *The Oxford Dictionary of English Proverbs* quotes seventeenth-century fencing master Sir W. Hope as saying: 'What he doth, he doth by rule of thumb, and not by art.' There is no suggestion here that the phrase refers to any aspect of violence against wives.

Brewer's Dictionary of Phrase and Fable states that the phrase is 'in allusion to the use of the thumb for rough measurement'.

Did you know ...?

To get one's 'just desserts' means to get one's 'appropriate pudding'. To get one's 'just deserts' means to get due reward or punishment.

'Deserts', in this context, is derived from the verb 'to deserve', so it should only have one 's' in the middle. Though 'deserts' is pronounced like the pudding, its spelling matches its originating verb.

'Scot free' derives from Scots getting away with things

To get off 'scot free' means to get away without paying the price, which is commonly assumed to be a jibe at the good people of Scotland.

Brewer's Dictionary of Phrase and Fable states that a 'scot' is a 'payment or reckoning'. The word first appeared in 1297 and is thought to derive from the Old Norse *skot* and the Old French *escot*, both meaning 'tax'. *The Oxford Dictionary of Proverbs* defines the term 'scot free' as meaning 'free from payment of scot, tavern score, fine etc.'.

To do something 'off one's own back' is to do something on one's own initiative

I was interested to read in a conservationist's press release recently, about a bat conservationist doing 'most of his bat work off his own back', when strictly speaking, he should be doing his bat work 'off his own bat'.

The phrase 'off one's own back' is an understandable mishearing of the correct form 'off one's own bat'.

It is, of course, of cricketing origin. Nothing to do with flying mammals.

To 'eat humble pie' derives from the verb 'to be humble'

Until the seventeenth century 'umbles' or 'numbles' were offal, from the Latin *lumulus*. 'Umble pie', therefore, was offal pie.

Umble   Humble

The seventeenth-century diarist Samuel Pepys records on 8 July 1663: 'Mrs Turner came in, and did bring us an umble pie hot out of her oven, extraordinary good.' It would seem that Pepys didn't appear too grand to 'eat umble pie'.

However, in the early 1800s the phrase became confused with the verb 'humble', which means 'close to the ground' and comes from the Latin *humilis*. To 'eat humble pie' became associated with 'submitting to humiliation' and continues to be regarded as such today.

Offal pie, anyone?

To wait with 'baited breath' means to wait with anxiety or excitement

In literal terms, to wait with 'baited breath' would mean hanging around with a mouth full of maggots. Not a pleasant thought.

This spelling of 'baited' comes from 'to bait', meaning 'to tease' or 'trap'. 'Bated', however, comes from 'to abate' which means 'to lessen'.

To 'bate' or 'abate' one's breath means to restrain one's breathing through anxiety or suspense. The correct spelling of the verb in the phrase, therefore, should be to wait with 'bated breath'.

20

Bodies

A sneeze stops the heart, which is why we say 'Bless you'

If this were so, many of us would be taking our lives into our hands every time we caught a cold, but is there any truth in the saying? BBC Radio Four's *Case Notes* presenter Dr Mark Porter thinks not. Though he says that it's true that 'cardiac output may be temporarily reduced due to increased pressure in the chest reducing venous return and right atrial filling pressure,' for all non-medical students that still means 'No.'

Dr Tom Wilson of the Washington University School of Medicine confirms that the 'heart is a big mass of electrically active tissue, and this electrical activity will not stop because of a sneeze', and suggests that next time we sneeze we should check our pulse to prove it.

But why do we say 'Bless you' when someone sneezes? First-century natural historian Pliny reveals that the 'salute' made when somebody sneezed was originally 'an observation which Tiberius Caesar, they say, the most unsociable of men . . . used to exact, when riding in his chariot'. While doing the rounds among his subjects it would appear that grumpy old Tiberius Caesar would insist the populace bless him if he should sneeze.

In his book *Pseudoxia Epidemica*, seventeenth-century doctor Sir Thomas Browne has much to say on the matter and suggests the custom was probably to ward off illness: 'Concerning Sternutation or Sneezing, and the custome of saluting or blessing upon that motion, it is pretended, and generally beleeved to derive its originall from a disease, wherein Sternutation proved mortall, and such as Sneezed dyed.'

Dr Wilson puts forward another explanation for the practice, namely that in earlier times, when a person sneezed it was thought that their 'soul might escape, or demons and evil spirits might get in', hence the need for a blessing to counter any negative effects of the sneeze.

Bad singers are 'tone deaf'

The *Oxford English Dictionary* defines 'tone deaf' as the inability to 'perceive differences of musical pitch accurately'. However, when I sing out of tune I know I'm hitting the wrong notes, I just don't know how to hit the right ones.

It appears that true 'tone deafness' is rare. Voice coach Roger Love claims in his book *Sing Like the Stars!* that less than 2 per cent of the population is actually tone deaf.

Indeed, vocal coach and author of *The Professional Singer's Handbook* Gloria Rusch believes that there is no such thing as a tone-deaf singer, and that anyone who appears to be so is 'merely one who is not hearing and distinguishing pitches well'. She explains that 'a good teacher can train someone to hear the notes correctly through use of the right scales and technique.'

We only use 10 per cent of our brains

The origins of this fallacy may well date back to 1935, when, according to Dr Nadine M. Weidman, scientist Karl Spencer Lashley had been experimenting on rats and concluded that 'as much as half the cerebrum [main part of the brain] could be destroyed without markedly affecting the rat's ability to learn.'

It is therefore believed that these early studies may have contributed to the theory that humans don't use or need all of their brains. The belief is often cited as proof that we have more mental abilities than we realize or that the 'dormant' portion of our brains must therefore have 'psychic' potential.

Professor Chris Frith of the Wellcome Department of Imaging Neuroscience states that: 'The idea that we only use ten per cent of our brain is a myth. All our brain cells are active all the time even when we are asleep ... Damage to quite small areas of our brain can have devastating effects.' Indeed, how often do we hear a surgeon comment: 'He was shot through the head. Fortunately, the bullet entered the ninety per cent of the brain he doesn't use ...'

In his book *Bad Medicine* science writer Christopher Wanjek dates the first recorded incidence of the 10-per-cent saying to a 1944 advertisement for 'the Pelman Institute, which offered self-improvement courses', which he quotes as urging: 'What's holding you back? Just one fact – one scientific fact. That is all. Because, as Science says, you are using only one-tenth of your real brain-power!'

Since then, scientists' brains continued to work away at

full capacity, fortunately, and now, as Wanjek points out: 'CAT, PET, and MRI scans all prove that there are no inactive regions of the brain . . . not even during sleep.'

Women don't have an Adam's apple

The *Oxford English Dictionary* definition of the Adam's apple is 'the projection at the front of the neck which is formed by the thyroid cartilage of the larynx.'

Though it might seem as though the Adam's apple is an exclusively male part of the anatomy, biology professor and author of *Anatomy and Physiology the Easy Way*, I. Edward Alcamo, reassures us that it is simply 'more pronounced in adult males than adult females'. A browse through *Applied Radiological Anatomy* confirms that the female version 'is easily palpable [can be felt], but not visible'.

So women certainly do have Adam's apples, but they are less obvious: without them they would not be able to speak . . .

Serves you right for being greedy.

A drowning person bobs to the surface three times before going under

It's unclear how this dangerous myth came about, but childcare expert and author of *Your Growing Child* Penelope Leach dismisses it as 'total nonsense'. She stresses that if a child falls into deep water it is vital that you 'get him out the moment he appears . . . If you wait while he bobs around you may be too late.'

David Walker, Water and Leisure Information Officer for the Royal Society for the Prevention of Accidents (RoSPA) concurs: 'The belief that a drowning person bobs to the surface three times before going under is something that we would refute . . . We have looked at over six thousand cases of drowning, and according to our records none have returned any substantial evidence of the "three bobs" legend.'

Indeed, drowning can be sudden and silent. Aquatic safety consultant Dave Smith reveals that 'drowning occurs rapidly and soundlessly, averaging twenty seconds in small children and up to a minute in adults.'

According to Walker: 'There are numerous cases of "cold-water shock syndrome" whereby even experienced watersports enthusiasts have drowned upon immediately entering the water.' In other words, in the time it might take you to decide whether someone might be in a spot of difficulty, they've probably already drowned.

On a rather tragic note, Walker adds that 'it would be more accurate to say that drowning people bob only once: just before they are rescued or helped out of the water. If they bob a second time – it's when their bodies are recovered after death.' A sobering thought indeed.

There are four tastes which can only be detected on specific sections of the tongue

It has long been considered that the tongue has four taste sensations due to having receptors that have specific topographical distribution – salt and sweet are deemed to be at the tip of the tongue, bitter is at the base, and acid or sour along the borders – and on one occasion at school, my class conducted an experiment to prove this. We dripped salt water, syrup, lemon juice and something that smelt of pear drops on to different sections of each others' tongues all afternoon. The result? Thirty-two very sticky schoolchildren.

We needn't have bothered. According to the findings of biology professor Donald C. Rizzo in *Delmar's Fundamentals of Anatomy and Physiology*:

All taste buds can detect all four sensations.' Furthermore, science writer Christopher Wanjek points out that 'the ubiquitous tongue map . . . is based on a hundred-year-old misinterpretation . . . Scientists misinterpreted Hanig's (1901) and Boring's (1945) work [tongue-taste research] and assumed areas of lower sensitivity were areas of no sensitivity.

Taste buds aren't only confined to the tongue. Publishing their findings in the *Journal of Applied Physiology*, researchers R. I. Henkin and R. L. Christiansen found that 'taste buds on the tongue, palate and pharynx [the cavity behind the nose and mouth that connects them to the oesophagus]' also detect 'all four modalities of taste'.

As for there being four discernible types of taste, anatomist Gerard J. Tortora points out in his book *Principles of Anatomy and Physiology* that 'five primary tastes can be distinguished: sour, sweet, bitter, salty, and umami.' Umami has recently been added to the list by Japanese scientists and is described as 'meaty' or 'savoury'.

Did you know ...?

Contortionists, who are performers capable of squeezing themselves into tiny boxes, and bending their bodies into unnatural shapes, are said to be able to do so because they are 'double-jointed'. Of course, they aren't!

The *Oxford Companion to the Body* tells us simply that 'these individuals do not have "double" joints, but they have a greater than average range of joint mobility' – the correct medical term being 'joint hypermobility'.

People from China and Japan cannot pronounce the letters 'r' or 'l'

The northern Chinese (mainly Mandarin speakers), including the people of Beijing and Shanghai, roll the letter 'r' as if they hailed from Birmingham. It is the Southern Chinese (mainly Cantonese speakers) and the Japanese who have trouble with 'r' and 'l', but not because they cannot pronounce them.

At birth, our brains are acutely receptive to the sounds of our own language, and, as graduate student in the

Neuroscience Program at Stanford University Gargi Talukder has explained in *How the Brain Learns a Second Language*, after a while our brains cease to register 'phonemes [speech sounds] that are not essential to the native language'.

Victoria and Robert Rodman, authors of *An Introduction to Language,* reveal that speakers who cannot clearly hear the difference between similar phonemes substitute another 'because of the acoustic similarity of these sounds'.

Having learned English in adulthood, foreign speakers who don't have the same sounds in their native language have trouble detecting the difference in two very similar speech sounds. They cannot easily discern a distinction between the two, and so are not able to tell if they have the pronunciation correct.

21

A Way With Words

'Forlorn Hope' soldiers were so named because they had no hope of success

The 'Forlorn Hope' is a body of troops chosen to spearhead an attack, and though these troops may well have had a limited life expectancy, that's not how the phrase came about.

The Concise Oxford Dictionary defines forlorn as 'miserable', 'lonely', 'forsaken' or 'sad'. The term dates back to the sixteenth century and comes from the Dutch *Verloren Hoop,* which means 'lost troop'. The fact that *Verloren Hoop* sounds like 'Forlorn Hope' is a strange coincidence.

The Forlorn Hope soldiers weren't as victimized as they sound, as the troop was sometimes made up from disgraced officers who were given a chance to win back their honour by being permitted to volunteer for a mission with little hope of success. They were often rewarded handsomely, if victorious, receiving promotions and monetary payments.

Posh stands for 'Port Side Out, Starboard Side Home'

During the nineteenth century, when the wealthiest travellers sailed to India with P&O (Peninsula and Orient), they requested the shady port side (left) when travelling out and the cool starboard side (right) when coming home. The acronym 'P.O.S.H.' is said to have been printed on their tickets. Indeed, it's even immortalized in the song 'POSH' from MGM's 1968 film *Chitty Chitty Bang Bang*.

However, according to P&O historian and archivist Stephen Rabson: 'Although as an attractive legend on the Liberty Valance principle the company did, in past years, make extensive use of the supposed deviation of the word in its publicity material and histories, "POSH" is an old chestnut for which P&O has no documentary evidence whatever.'

The Bloomsbury Dictionary of Word Origins suggests that 'posh' may have gained its meaning from the Romany word 'posh', which originally meant 'half' and became slang for 'money'.

Vertigo is a fear of heights

According to the *Concise Oxford English Dictionary*, vertigo is defined as 'a sensation of whirling and a tendency to lose balance; dizziness, giddiness'.

It comes from the Latin *vertere* which means 'turn'. The correct term for the fear of heights is acrophobia, which comes from the Greek *akron* meaning 'peak'.

Vertigo can be a symptom of acrophobia, but it is quite possible to suffer from vertigo at ground level, for example, when stepping off a playground roundabout.

Eskimos have four hundred words for snow

Linguistics professor and author of *The Great Eskimo Vocabulary Hoax,* Geoffrey K. Pullum, reveals that 'Eskimos do not have lots of different words for snow, and no one who knows anything about Eskimos . . . has ever said they do.'

Pullum suggests that the misconception may date back to a 1940s article, 'Science and Linguistics', by linguist Benjamin Lee Whorf who, quoting the work of anthropologist Franz Boas, loosely made the implication. The myth then snowballed (sorry!). According to Pullum: 'The four hundred figure came from a piece by a would-be author who admitted (under questioning by a magazine fact-checker) to having no source for the number whatsoever.'

Setting the record straight, Pullum suggests that the Central Alaskan Yup'ik Eskimo language has 'about a dozen words (even a couple of dozen if you are fairly liberal about what you count) for referring to snow and to related natural phenomena, events, or behaviour'.

Margarine should be pronounced with a soft 'g'

The forerunner of artificial butter was discovered in 1813. The fat-like substance was named 'margaric acid' from the Greek word for 'pearl' because the substance formed pearls of fatty acid. The name 'Margaret' (which also means pearl) comes from the same source.

'Oleomargarine' or 'pearly oil' was invented in 1860 and shortened to 'margarine' but, like Margaret, it was pronounced with a hard 'g'. The 1926 edition of *Fowler's Modern English Usage* claimed that the pronunciation with a soft 'g' was 'clearly wrong'. However, the modern edition of *Fowler's* rightly points out that the soft 'g' pronunciation has become 'overwhelmingly dominant'.

Bikinis are named after a two-piece atoll in the Pacific

The only problem is that Bikini Atoll consists of a ring of up to thirty-six small coral islands; it is not a two-piece atoll.

In an article for *Eye* magazine, writer Steven Heller reveals that a 'French bathing-suit designer, Louis Réard, took the name "bikini" from the Marshall Islands where two American atom bombs were tested in 1946', and describes how, in a fit of bad taste, Réard named his creation 'bikini', 'because he thought that the name signified the explosive effect that the suit would have on men'. Réard later claimed he named the sunwear after the islands and not the explosion.

'Sirloin' steak is so called because it was knighted

According to seventeenth-century British scholar Thomas Fuller, writing in *The Church History of Britain from the Birth of Jesus Christ until the Year 1648,*

Now it's 'Sir Sausage' and 'Sir Haddock'...

the sirloin steak was so named because it was 'knighted, saith tradition, by this King Henry [VIII]'.

Tradition saith wrong, as *Fowler's Modern English Usage* explains that 'evidence has survived falsely attributing the "knighting" of a loin of beef'.

'Sirloin' comes from the French *sur* meaning 'above', and *loigne* or *longe* meaning 'loin', which produces 'above the loin'.

'Jealousy' is the desire to possess what someone else has

As *The Good Word Guide* points out, jealousy is 'a concern to avoid the loss of something that one regards as one's own.' For example, one might 'jealously guard' one's possessions.

The Good Word Guide also reveals that 'envy' is 'the awareness of an advantage possessed by someone else, together with a desire to have that advantage oneself.' Therefore, one might be 'envious' of another's possession or position, but not 'jealous' of it if one didn't have it in the first place.

Town criers used to call 'Oh yea! Oh yea! Oh yea!'

B efore the joys of electronic communication the town crier used to attract the attention of locals with a hearty, 'Oh yea! Oh yea! Oh yea!'

Oh no! Oh no! Oh no! That simply isn't so. The actual call is 'Oyez!' It just sounds like 'Oh yea!' St Albans town crier Martin Hallett explains that the cry is 'derived from the Old French expression for "Listen!" or "Hear Ye!"' *The Concise Oxford Dictionary of Word Origins* confirms that oyez (the imperative plural) is Anglo-Norman coming from the Old French *oïr* meaning 'to hear'. Hallett also explains that 'after the proclamation was read, the scroll was nailed to a post . . . hence the expression "to post a notice".'

To be on 'tenderhooks' means to be in a state of suspense

P hrases such as 'I left him on tenderhooks to know what he may find' are often found in print. The expression evokes an image of being hung up on painful hooks and though it's not so far from the reality, it's still wrong!

According to the *Oxford English Dictionary*, a 'tenter'

was 'a framework on which . . . cloth is stretched to dry'. Therefore, 'tenterhooks' were the hooks used to fasten the cloth to the frame.

The correct spelling of the word in the above phrase is 'tenterhooks'.

Did you know . . . ?

'Miniatures' are generally thought of as small paintings, but a miniature can be of any size. According to the *Encyclopaedia Britannica*, 'the name is derived from the "minium", or red lead, used by the medieval illuminators.'

Miniatura became associated with the painting rather than the process, and then came to mean the tiny portraits produced during the early sixteenth to the mid-nineteenth centuries.

S.O.S. is an acronym for 'Save Our Souls'

What does S.O.S. stand for? 'Save Our Ship' or 'Save Our Souls'?

The first distress call used by the Marconi Company was C.Q.D. The letters did indeed stand for something: C.Q. was a shortened expression of 'seek you', and D stood for danger or distress. They have also been interpreted as meaning 'Come Quickly: Danger.' However, in *The Ocean Almanac,* author Robert Hendrickson reveals that in 1908 'the letters S.O.S. were chosen simply because the Morse code for them (three dots, three dashes, three dots) was easy to remember and transmit'. In other words,

S.O.S. is not an acronym, it is simply a sequence of three letters which are easy to transmit in Morse.

Incidentally, the distress call, Mayday has nothing to do with the first of May. It derives from the French *m'aidez* – 'help me'.

'Re' is an abbreviation for 'referring to', or 'with regard to'

'Re' is invariably used to mean 'regarding', 'referring to' or 'with regard to'. On the strength of this, 're' is understandably thought to be a simple abbreviation for 'regarding' or 'referring to'. However, it isn't a literal abbreviation for either of these words.

Fowler's Modern English Usage explains that 're' comes from the Latin *res*, which simply means 'thing'. In correspondence, the word is short for the Latin phrase *in re*, which, according to the *OED*, originally meant 'in the matter of', and which in modern terms means 'in the legal case of' or 'with regard to'. It is simply a coincidence that 're' and the two modern words with which it has come to be most associated – 'regarding' and 'reference' – both begin with the same two letters.

'Scotch' is an incorrect term to describe Scots

The people of Scotland are 'Scots' never 'Scotch'. But it hasn't always been so.

In 1786, Scottish poet Robert Burns wrote: 'Songs in the English language, if by Scotchmen, are admitted, but the music must be all Scotch.' While in 1829, Edinburgh-born novelist and poet Sir Walter Scott wrote in *Rob Roy*: 'At the first Scotch town which we reached, my guide sought out his friend and counsellor.'

Fowler's Modern English Usage quotes A. J. Aitken as stating: 'For working-class Scots the common form has long been Scotch . . . and the native form Scots is sometimes regarded as an Anglicized affectation.' Indeed, the word 'Scots' is generally considered to be an English contraction of the word 'Scottish'. However, *Fowler's* goes on to remind us that in modern-day Scotland, 'Scotch' is likely to be regarded as 'droll' or 'improper'.

The word now lives on only in terms such as Scotch egg, Scotch broth, Scotch whisky and Scotch mist.

Xmas is a disrespectful way to write Christmas

At school, my religious-education teacher expressly forbade us to write 'Xmas'. It was regarded as a foul blasphemy. How would I like it if people used an anonymous 'x' in place of my name? However, it would seem that the word 'Xmas' is not blasphemous after all.

In the original Greek, 'Christ' was written 'Xristos', but the 'x' isn't the Roman 'ecks'; *The Cassell Dictionary of Word Histories* explains that it is the Greek letter 'chi' (pronounced with a 'k' to rhyme with 'eye' – k'eye). The 'x' is simply a stand-in for 'the first letter of Greek Khristos – Christ'. Indeed, the Chi-Rho (Ch-r – the first two syllables of 'Christ') illumination can be seen in the ancient Irish manuscript of the Gospels, *The Book of Kells,* which is housed at Trinity

College in Dublin. This work dates back to the ninth century.

Of course, strictly speaking, 'Xmas' should still be pronounced 'Christmas' because it's an abbreviation, not an alternative word.

The Final Fallacy

Definitions are definitive

Select Bibliography

Ayto, John, *Bloomsbury Dictionary of Word Origins* (Bloomsbury, 1990)

Blakemore, Colin and others, *The Oxford Companion to the Body* (Oxford University Press, 2002)

Burchfield, R. W. (ed.), *The New Fowler's Modern English Usage* (OUP, 1996)

Burnam, Tom, *The Dictionary of Misinformation* (Crowell, 1975)

Burnam, Tom, *More Misinformation* (Crowell, 1980)

Cobham Brewer, E., Room, Adrian (eds) *Brewer's Dictionary of Phrase and Fable*, 15th edn (HarperResource, 1995)

Davidson, Alan, *The Oxford Companion to Food* (OUP, 1999)

Fowler, H. W. and others, *Concise Oxford English Dictionary* (OUP, 2003)

Hendrickson, Robert, *The Ocean Almanac* (Main Street, 1984)

Hoad, T. F. (ed.), *The Concise Oxford Dictionary of English Etymology* (OUP, 1966)

Hoad, T. F. (ed.), *The Concise Oxford Dictionary of Word Origins* (OUP, 1986)

Hoad, T. F. (ed.), *The Oxford Library of Words and Phrases* (OUP, 1993)

Manser, Martin H. (ed.), *The Good Word Guide* (Bloomsbury, 1992)

Room, Adrian, *The Cassell Dictionary of Word Histories* (Cassell & Co., 2000)

Siefring, Judith, *The Oxford Dictionary of Idioms* (OUP, 2004)

Soanes, Catherine, Stevenson, Angus (eds), *Oxford Dictionary of English* (OUP, 2001)

Tuleja, Tad, *Fabulous Fallacies* (The Stonesong Press, 1982)

Wanjek, Christopher, *Bad Medicine: Misconceptions and Misuses Revealed, from Distance Healing to Vitamin O* (Wiley, 2002)

Ward, Philip, *A Dictionary of Common Fallacies* (Oleander Press, 1978)

Wilson, F. P., *The Oxford Dictionary of English Proverbs* (Clarendon Press, 1980)

Useful websites

www.britannica.com
www.madsci.org
www.findagrave.com
www.findadeath.com
www.rethink.org
www.army.mod.uk
www.nhsdirect.nhs.uk

All other references to source material can be found within the individual entries in each chapter.